Board Book *Play*
EASY TECHNIQUES FROM A TO Z

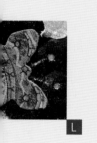

Text & Artwork © 2006 C&T Publishing, Inc.

Publisher: Amy Marson

Editorial Director: Gailen Runge

Editor: Mary Wruck

Copyeditor/Proofreader: Wordfirm Inc.

Design Director: Christina D. Jarumay

Cover & Book Designer: Christina D. Jarumay

Illustrator: Tim Manibusan

Production Assistant: Zinnia Heinzmann

Photography: Luke Mulks

Published by C&T Publishing, Inc., P.O. Box 1456, Lafayette, CA 94549

Library of Congress Cataloging-in-Publication Data

Board book play : easy techniques from A to Z.

   p. cm.

  ISBN-13: 978-1-57120-407-3 (paper trade : alk. paper)

  ISBN-10: 1-57120-407-5 (paper trade : alk. paper)

  1. Photograph albums. 2. Scrapbooks. 3. Decoration and ornament. I.

Title.

  TR501.B63 2006

  745.593–dc22

        2006012943

Printed in China

10 9 8 7 6 5 4 3 2 1

Contents

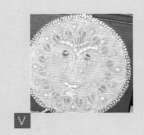

INTRODUCTION...4

EASY TECHNIQUES FROM A TO Z

Introduction

Ready-To-Go! Blank Board Books available from C&T Publishing.

There's nothing like a personalized Board Book to capture all the special moments of your life. Whether you treasure it, display it, or gift it, with the techniques found in this book you'll learn how to make your Board Book as unique as you are. Try any of the more than 30 different techniques from 36 experts who are celebrated as the most talented and creative designers in their field. Discover how to create and use:

- Surface treatments like painting, batik, and decoupage
- Embellishments like jewels, mirrors, and frames
- Enhancements like journaling, recipes, and quotations

Need help finding tools and supplies? There's a complete directory of resources provided beginning on page 79. Visit www.blankboardbooks.com or your favorite craft store to check out all of C&T Publishing's *Ready-To-Go! Blank Board Book* shapes, colors, and sizes—there's sure to be a book that's perfect for your project!

EASY TECHNIQUES
from A *to* Z

A is for Acetate Overlays

Roots

BY BETH HOOPER

Transparent elements give amazing depth to a photo album. Create multiple layers with papers under the photos, then add pictures, and finish with acetate overlays, transparencies, and epoxy stickers. With all the overlapping and the see-through layers, the effect is really three-dimensional.

SUPPLIES:

- 6″× 6″ Create & Treasure Ready-To-Go! Blank Board Book, white (C&T Publishing)
- Patterned papers with vintage look (Mustard Moon, Daisy D's)
- Laser copies of old photos
- Transparencies and epoxy stickers, Narratives by Karen Russell (Creative Imaginations)
- Decorative clip (EK Success)
- Large sticker letters (Mustard Moon)
- Red gingham fabric strip, 1″× 20″
- Manila tags or file folder
- Safety pin
- Walnut ink spray or distress ink pad, vintage photo color (Ranger)
- Adhesive: your choice for papers; Diamond Glaze for transparent items (JudiKins)
- Fine sandpaper; Scuffers (Lasting Impressions)
- Sharp scissors

INSTRUCTIONS:

1. Glue the patterned papers in related designs and colors to cover all the pages and the cover of the book.

2. Make pleasant arrangements of the photos on the pages, leaving some blank spaces, and glue them down.

3. Add transparencies, trimming as needed to avoid covering faces in photos. If the photos are not self-stick, glue them down with Diamond Glaze.

4. Type or print photo information on manila tags or a folder. Dampen and wipe on ink to age them, then cut out.

5. Add sticker motifs, letters, and words to fill spaces. Vary type style and size for interest.

6. Sand the edges of the pages for a distressed look to contrast with the sharpness of the transparencies.

7. Fray the edges of the fabric strip by pulling out strings along the edge.

8. Wipe the tag edges and gingham strip with ink to age them.

9. Run the gingham strip through the spine of the book, pushing it through with a skewer or pencil. Tie the ends on the outside of the spine.

10. Add transparency and letter stickers to the tag and pin it onto the gingham knot.

A is for Art Doll

Junk Food, Flat Women

BY ELINOR PEACE BAILEY

Art dolls are not commercial creations but are born from the hands of their maker. Each is a unique creation, so there is no need to make your interpretation look exactly like this one. The Blank Board Book forms the body, and the arms, legs, and head shapes are cut from snack-food boxes. The people spring out and wave as you turn the pages—have fun with this "moving" experience.

SUPPLIES:

- 3″ × 3″ Create & Treasure Ready-To-Go! Blank Board Book, black (C&T Publishing)

- Templates of doll legs, arms, etcetera (provided)

- Colorful snack-food boxes or other chipboard, poster board, or recycled packaging

- Small hole punch (strong enough to punch cardboard)

- Brads: stars or other large-headed shapes to match the spirit of your art doll

- Sharp scissors

- Colorful permanent markers, paint pens, glitter glue, and/or other embellishments

INSTRUCTIONS:

1. Trace the patterns and use them to cut out the arms, legs, and heads from the cardboard. Or you can cut your own shapes using the photos and patterns as inspiration. If the cardboard is already patterned, you don't have to trace the features of the body parts.

2. Punch holes in the arms, legs, and heads as shown on the patterns.

3. Punch corresponding holes in the book pages where the body parts will stick out of the pages, varying their positions on the pages for interest.

4. Attach the body parts to the pages by running brads through holes in the page and the body part.

5. Add words or decorations with paint pens, permanent markers, or glitter glue.

B is for Batik

Inspiration Book

BY DELORES RUZICKA

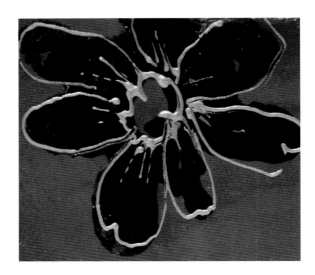

SUPPLIES:

- 3″ × 3″ Create & Treasure Ready-To-Go! Blank Board Book, black (C&T Publishing)

- Batik EZ (Crafter's Pick)

- Decoupage and Collage Gel (Crafter's Pick)

- Foam stamps, your choice of designs

- ColorArtz acrylic spray paints (Testors)

- DecoArt Paper Effects paint, silver pearl

- Soft Comfort Series 14550, batik ¾″ wash brush (Loew-Cornell)

- Computer

- Cardstock, ecru

- Paint tray

- Sponge

INSTRUCTIONS:

1. Lay the mini book flat on your work surface. Begin with the front and back covers of the book, then continue the following process on the inside of the book, working both the left and right pages at the same time with the same design and color.

2. Pour a small puddle of Batik EZ (about the size of a quarter) onto a tray. If the Batik EZ is very thick, add a little water and mix until it is of a thick, syrupy consistency.

3. Use the ¾″ brush to apply an even coat of Batik EZ onto a foam stamp. Press the stamp onto the mini book. Repeat this step in a random fashion. You don't have to let the Batik EZ dry.

4. Spray on an even, light application of acrylic paint in the color of your choice (spray over the top of the Batik EZ stampings). As soon as the paint is dry, use a wet sponge to remove the Batik EZ; this will create the batik effects.

5. Repeat this process with each page, using the foam stamp and the color of paint of your choice. Let dry.

6. Using the DecoArt Paper Effects paint, outline the batik images on each page. Allow drying time before proceeding to the next page. This will eliminate smudging.

7. Use your computer to print words such as *Inspiration*, *Dance*, and *Sing* on the cardstock.

8. Tear the paper around each word, creating a deckled edge, and glue each word to the desired cover or inside page.

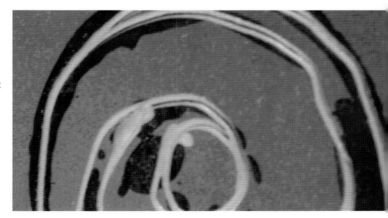

C is for Cheers

The Little Book of Cheer

BY KATIE WATSON

This little Board Book is chock full of cheers! It provides a handy reference for just the right toast to use on almost any occasion. Adding it to a decorated wine-bottle holder makes it a gift to remember.

SUPPLIES:

- 3″ × 3″ Create & Treasure Ready-To-Go! Blank Board Book, white (C&T Publishing)

- Patterned papers: red gingham and other assorted patterns

- Rub-on letters

- Letter stamps

- Cardstock

- Computer (to create toasts)

- Ribbon

- Charms

- Mini safety pin

- Brads

- Mod Podge (Plaid)

- Paper piercer

INSTRUCTIONS:

Cover

1. Decoupage the front and back covers with patterned paper cut into a 2½″ × 2½″ square. Be sure to glue it so that the spine of the book is left uncovered.

2. Mat a strip of red gingham–patterned paper with white cardstock and glue to the bottom of the front cover.

3. Make the title using stamps, stickers, and/or rub-on letters.

4. Add embellishment stickers.

Inside Pages

1. Using decoupage, cover the pages with patterned papers, being sure to leave a tiny border around all four edges of each page.

2. Add strips of coordinating patterned paper, alternating patterns across the tops and bottoms of each page.

3. Stamp the desired word across the top of the page and across the strip of patterned paper.

4. Add a piece of cardstock, preprinted with the toast on it, to the center of the page.

5. Add embellishment stickers to fill open areas on the page.

Closure

1. Using the paper piercer, make a hole in the front and back covers right in the middle, at the outer edge. Be sure not to make it too close to the edge; otherwise the brad will tear through.

2. Push the prongs of a large brad through the hole and spread them out on the back of the next page.

3. Wrap a thin ribbon around the base of the brad on the back page. Tie it into a knot at the base of the head and snip off the extra ribbon. Be sure to leave the rest of the ribbon intact.

4. Take the ribbon from the back brad and pull it around to the front brad, wrapping it several times around the base of the head to close the book.

Finishing

1. Loop a ribbon through the spine of the book and tie it in a double knot. Snip the edges at an angle.

2. Attach a charm with the mini safety pin.

3. Tie the mini book around the neck of a wine bottle or attach it to a decoupaged wine-bottle gift box for a great gift!

D is for Decoupage

My Family

BY SUE ELDRED

Recently, I had the privilege of helping my parents sort through old boxes of inherited photos and listening to much forgotten family trivia. "My Family" album uses decoupage, a technique whereby you apply assorted papers and cutouts and then coat everything with multiple layers of varnish. I made this album as a tribute to my parents on their 50th wedding anniversary. What a wonderful and loving couple they are. Thanks, Mom and Dad.

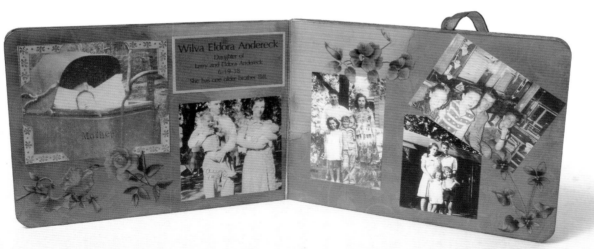

SUPPLIES:

- 7˝ × 5˝ Create & Treasure Ready-To-Go! Blank Board Book, white (C&T Publishing)

- Decorative papers: Secret Garden (Daisy D's); green damask, plum and olive diamonds, purple parchment, Brenda Walton's Bella acorn (K&Co.); iridescent vellum (Paper Cut); miscellaneous green-striped papers

- Stickers: Henry's Lace (Mrs. Grossman's); Garden Collage Frames (K&Co.); Sandy Clough Heirloom Garden (Colorbök)

- Victoriana photo corners (Frances Meyer)

- Archival ink, sepia (Ranger)

- Hydro sponge

- Foam brush

- Liquid Laminate (Beacon)

- Craft Bond Tacky Glue (Elmer's)

- Ribbon (May Arts)

- X-Acto knife

- Cutting mat

- Red rubber brayer

- ⅛˝ utility hole punch (McGill)

- Xyron sticker machine

- Bone folder

INSTRUCTIONS:

1. Using sepia ink and a hydro sponge, gently rub ink onto the outside edges of the book and the inside creases of the pages.

2. Cut two pieces of Secret Garden or other decorative paper to 7″× 5″. Apply a thin layer of glue with a small foam brush and glue the paper to the front and back of the book. (A red rubber brayer is good for securing the paper firmly.) Trim the paper from around the corners with the X-Acto knife.

3. Cut a small strip of green damask or other colored paper to approximately 4″× 7″. Center around the spine of the book and gently make score lines. Fold on the score lines. Apply glue and paste the paper to the end of the book.

4. Add decorative lace stickers to the front and back covers of the book.

5. Gently rub sepia ink onto the front and back covers to give them an aged look.

6. Add a *Family* sticker to the top right corner of the book.

7. Add a thin layer of Liquid Laminate to the front and back of the book. Let dry thoroughly and repeat two or three times, as desired.

8. The inside pages are done the same way as in Step 2. Use a bone folder to gently rub the inside edges of the book.

9. Use traditional scrapbooking techniques to decorate the pages, such as applying torn paper, photo corners, computer-generated journaling, and old family photos.

10. If you want to soften the look of the pages, as on *The Wedding* page, use an additional sheet of vellum and run the vellum through the Xyron sticker machine. Then apply and decorate as usual.

11. To tie up the book, punch a ⅛″ hole in the top and bottom of the back cover, and string the ribbon through to tie around the front of the book.

E is for Embellishments

Winged Ancestors

BY MARGERT ANN KRULJAC

This lovely little fantasy book can easily be created with a few simple embellishments. It's a fun way to pretend that our ancestors just might have had wings.

SUPPLIES:

- 3″ × 3″ Create & Treasure Ready-To-Go! Blank Board Book, black (C&T Publishing)
- Patterned papers (K&Co., BasicGrey)
- Girl images (art-e-zine, Altered Pages)
- Butterfly sticker (PSX)
- Jewels (Kandi)
- Glitter (Art Institute)

- Wire
- Awl
- Large snap (Prym Consumer USA)
- Word and definition stickers (Die Cuts With A View)
- Letter stamps (Image Tree)
- Ornament stamp
- Alcohol inks (Ranger)

- Adornaments fibers (EK Success)
- Ribbon (Offray)
- Mod Podge (Plaid)
- Ultimate! adhesive (Crafter's Pick)
- Ink, jet black, StazOn (Tsukineko)
- Feather (Zucker)
- Flowers

INSTRUCTIONS:

Cover

1. Glue patterned paper to front and back covers with Mod Podge and trim to size.

2. Paint Mod Podge over the flowers on the bottom of the girl's dress and sprinkle glitter onto the flowers. Shake off excess.

3. Paste the girl's image to the top of the butterfly sticker and then glue jewels to the butterfly wings.

4. Paste the butterfly to the front cover.

5. With an awl, poke small holes into the hat on the girl's head; thread wire through the holes and shape into an antenna.

6. Place the word sticker *Ancestors* along the binding edge.

7. Stamp the word *Winged* onto the lower right-hand side.

8. Color the large snap with alcohol inks and attach an 8˝ piece of ribbon.

9. Glue the top part of the snap to the edge of the front cover.

10. Repeat Steps 8 and 9 for the bottom part of the snap, which goes on the back cover.

> **NOTE:**
>
> *The snap is for adornment and will not be used to snap the book closed. The ribbons attached to the snap parts will be used to tie the book closed.*

11. Poke a hole in the spine of the book and thread assorted fibers through the hole.

Inside Pages

1. Glue patterned paper to each side of the spread with Mod Podge and trim away excess.

2. Cut out the girl's image and glue feathers and fibers to her back to form wings using Ultimate! adhesive.

3. Paste the image to the left-hand page of the spread.

4. Place the *Heart* definition sticker across the spread.

5. Glue flowers to the bottom of the right-hand page and then glue jewels to the flower centers. Using black ink, stamp the decorative ornament stamp at the top of the same page.

F

F is for Fancy Frames

Treasures of the Heart

BY SUE ELDRED

I made this necklace using a coordinated palette of cream and black scrapbooking products for a classy and cohesive look; then I added a hint of shabby chic and vintage memorabilia for fun. Sweet verses make this project truly a treasure of the heart. The metal frame on the cover holds an aged photo of the Eiffel Tower, while an inside photo pocket frames another vintage image. Simple techniques make this a fun project for both beginning and experienced paper crafters.

SUPPLIES:

- 3″× 3″ Create & Treasure Ready-To-Go! Blank Board Book, black (C&T Publishing)

- Patterned papers: black and beige polka dot, Brianna text and botanicals, Brianna block collage, gold floral, Life's Journey stamp collection, black gingham (K&Co.); cream roses (Anna Griffin)

- Stickers: Brenda Walton's Maison Towering type, embossed floral ivory borders (K&Co.)

- Beyond Postmarks large metal frames, silver (K&Co.)

- Life's Journey vintage compass charm (K&Co.)

- Brenda Walton's Quotable Notables vellum expressions and sayings (K&Co.)

- Tools: mini envelope punch; 1⅞″ deckle stacking square punch; ⅛″ utility hole punch; ⅛″ paper drill (McGill)

- Super Tape acid-free double-sided adhesives, ⅛″ and ¼″ (Therm O Web)

- Liquid Laminate (Beacon)

- Archival inks: sepia, Tim Holtz black soot (Ranger)

- Ribbon (May Arts)

- Craft Bond Fabric and Paper Glue, Craft Bond Tacky Glue (Elmer's)

- Matte finish spray (Krylon)

- Acrylic paint, antique white (Plaid)

- Gold metallic slivers (Mrs. Grossman's)

- Xyron sticker machine

- Foam brush

- Red rubber brayer

INSTRUCTIONS:

Cover

1. Cut two pieces of cream roses paper 3″ square. Apply glue with a foam brush and paste the paper to the front and back covers of the book. Use the red rubber brayer to secure the paper firmly.

2. Cut a strip of polka-dot paper to 1¼″× 3″. Score ½″ lengthwise on both sides, fold on the score lines, and glue to the book's spine. Add metallic slivers to the edges of the paper.

3. Paint the silver frame with two coats of vintage white paint; then rub black soot ink with your fingertip over the raised areas of the frame. If these areas then seem too dark, rub a little additional cream paint onto the frame.

4. Give the frame an antiqued look by gently rubbing it with a small amount of sepia ink.

5. Spray the frame with matte finish sealer to set the inks. Paint on a thin layer of Liquid Laminate and let dry thoroughly.

6. Apply ⅛″ Super Tape around the inside opening of the frame and insert the Eiffel Tower sticker, leaving the protective sticker coating in place.

7. Add ¼″ tape around the back of the frame. Remove the protective coating from the tape, take the back off the Eiffel Tower sticker, and adhere it onto the front of the book.

8. Tie a small piece of ribbon to the compass charm and glue it to the front of the frame.

9. Punch a ⅛″ hole into the front and back covers of the book. Add ribbons for a closure.

10. Drill a ⅛″ hole into the top left corner of the book, going through all the pages. Loop a thin ribbon through the hole, add a coordinating bead, and tie a knot at the end to make the necklace.

Inside Pages

1. Run the vellum sayings through the Xyron sticker machine.

2. Apply a sheet of decorative paper to each page, cutting it to fit the page. Paste paper to the inside of the book with a thin coat of glue.

3. Punch a mini envelope shape from the gold floral paper. Fold down the sides. Apply glue to the side edges of the front flap only and set aside.

4. Apply two strips of cream embossed stickers to the top and bottom of the page. For an antiqued look, gently rub a small amount of sepia ink onto the raised surfaces of the stickers.

5. Punch a deckle square from patterned paper and paste it to the center of the page. The square should be turned sideways on the page to form a diamond shape, as pictured.

6. Cut a small picture of children from the Life's Journey stamp collection and glue it to the back of a small piece black gingham paper. Trim around the picture and insert it into the mini envelope. Paste the envelope with the picture tucked inside to the top of the deckled square.

7. Add an embellishment sticker to the top of the mini envelope.

G is for Glazing

Dreams of Inspiration

BY LEA CIOCI

Glazing is a good way to create layers of color, some sheerer than others, depending on the look you want to achieve. Aging or antiquing lend themselves amazingly to this project by using glazing to build up color. The Board Book is magically transformed from a two-dimensional, flat look to an aged, in-depth, three-dimensional page reminiscent of a treasure one might find in an attic or an old trunk. The best part about glazing is playing. Be free with the colors as you put each layer down; this is what makes the antiquing look realistic.

SUPPLIES:

- 7″ × 5″ Create & Treasure Ready-To-Go! Blank Board Book, white (C&T Publishing)

- Paint: fresh foliage, pure gold (FolkArt Papier)

- Flow medium (FolkArt Papier)

- Distress inks: vintage photo, tea dye, mustard (Ranger)

- Assorted word stamps and scanned images

- Patterned papers (Design Originals)

- Copper hinge (EK Success)

- Bottle cap, bottle cap image, decorative slide mount, and mini tag (Design Originals)

- Metal words, metal heart shape, and die cuts (All My Memories)

- Copper fragments, metal pinwheels (Hot Off The Press)

- Die cut, collage, and epoxy stickers (K&Co.)

- Inkjet fabric (Vintage Workshop)

- Medium Craft Zots, Memory Tape Runner (Therm O Web)

- Aleene's Instant Decoupage glue (Duncan)

- Scissors

- Soft painting brushes, 1 large, 1 small

- Foam plates

- Small cloth or sponge

INSTRUCTIONS:

Basic Glazing and Cover

1. On a foam plate, mix a generous amount of fresh foliage paint with the flow medium. The flow medium thins the paint to a glaze consistency. Adding water would make the paint too thin and runny; the medium maintains the body of the paint. Paint all pages with this mixture. Let dry.

2. Mix a small amount of pure gold paint with the flow medium, as in Step 1. Using the small paintbrush, brush the color onto various areas of the pages. Let dry.

3. Starting with the mustard ink, do DTP (direct to paper) by lightly dragging the ink pad randomly over the surface of the page. Use a sponge to blend the color. Follow the same technique with the remaining colors of ink.

4. Tear a 1/2″ strip from the cover by ripping down. This is done to add dimension and allow the second page to show through.

5. Edge the ripped end of the cover with additional ink.

6. Affix the slide mount to the cover, using the tape runner. Paste the bottle cap in the center of the slide mount, using a Zot. Press the child's image into the center of the bottle cap.

7. Affix the mini tag using the tape runner. Glue a little charm in place with decoupage glue. Paste on the metal heart and metal word with a Zot.

Inside Pages

1. After glazing each page, stamp words on, using ink.

2. To create the pocket, cut a triangle of decorative paper to fit the inner edge of the page. Rip the left edge (the pocket opening) to give a textured look. Using decoupage glue, apply glue to only the cut edges and paste to book page. Add embellishments.

3. To create the fabric tag and word panel, first scan artwork into the computer and print it on inkjet fabric, then cut it out. Inkjet fabric has a paper backing, which is removed on the word panel but not on the tag. This allows the tag to be easily put into and taken out of the pocket.

4. For the page opposite the pocket page, rip decorative paper into a rectangular shape to fit within the page, leaving open a painted border of approximately 1 1/2″. Affix with decoupage glue. Add the die cuts and metal word. Do DTP with ink over the die cuts to give an aged look. Add word fragments.

5. Press the adhesive-backed hinge in place so that the right edge of the inkjet quote fabric is just under the hinge.

H is for Halloween Memento

Book of Boo

BY KATIE WATSON

This fun little Halloween memento book is guaranteed to bring out a little Halloween "Boo" spirit in you! Full of bright Halloween colors and patterns, it's sure to be a favorite treat for everyone in your family. Inside you'll find bats and cats, pumpkins, candy corn, and stars, all just waiting for a picture of your little one to make this Halloween mumm-er-y book complete.

SUPPLIES:

- 3″ × 3″ Create & Treasure Ready-To-Go! Blank Board Book, black (C&T Publishing)
- White cardstock (Bazzill)
- ColorBox black stamping ink (Clearsnap)
- Mini bottle-cap letters (Li'l Davis Designs)
- Plastic spider
- Wiggle eyes
- Alphabet beads
- Black-and-white gingham ribbon (Offray)

- Black embroidery thread (DMC)
- Floss threader (find in dental section of grocery store)
- Glue Dots
- Black-and-white gingham paper (Making Memories)
- Patterned paper: Black Star-Night Sky (KI Memories)
- Rickrack (May Arts)
- Rub-on bat and words (Making Memories)

- Spooky word metal signage (Making Memories)
- Paper cutter (EK Success)
- Mono-Multi liquid glue (Tombow)
- Scissors

INSTRUCTIONS:

Cover

1. Cut white textured cardstock into strips of different sizes the approximate width of the cover of the book. Ink the edges with black stamping ink. Glue the strips down across the cover of the book, gluing some down at an angle. Leave a space in the middle free of white cardstock so the black of the Board Book shows through (this will be for the eyes).

2. Glue down the wiggle eyes in the black space.

3. Feed the black-and-white gingham ribbon through the spine of the book using a floss threader. Tie the ribbon in a knot and snip the edges at an angle.

4. Thread black embroidery thread through the beads, spelling the word *Book* and tie a knot at both ends of the word to keep the beads stationary. Do the same thing with the letters spelling *Of*. Next, thread the embroidery thread through the spine of the book and tie it in a double or triple knot. Snip the ends close to the knot. Rotate the thread until the words are in the middle of the bookbinding.

5. Roll a couple of Glue Dots together to make a more dimensional Glue Dot ball with a wide base and glue the plastic spider to the front cover.

6. Paste the mini bottle-cap letters spelling the word *Boo* to the front cover in the same way you glued the spider.

Inside Pages

1. Cut black-and-white gingham paper 3″ x 3″ to fit the pages (as the base paper) and paste, using liquid glue.

2. Cut black star paper ¼″ smaller than the base paper and adhere. Some of the gingham paper from the base should be left showing.

3. Cut two strips of black-and-white gingham paper 3″ wide and paste one to each page.

4. Using black embroidery thread, tie a tag to the rickrack. Embellish the tag with a Halloween embellishment such as a bat rub-on.

5. Glue down pieces of rickrack on top of the gingham strips.

6. Add a Halloween embellishment or sticker to the top left corner of the left-hand page.

7. Glue in photos of your favorite pirates and ninja warriors.

Closure

1. Punch a hole in the center of the edge of both the front and back covers, making sure not to get too close to the edge. If the hole is too close to the edge, it will tear through.

2. Thread two pieces of gingham ribbon, one through each hole, and tie the inside into a knot so it won't slip through. Use these ribbons to tie the book closed.

Love never fails

I is for Inking

An Expression of Faith, Hope, and Love

BY TAMARA JOYCE-WYLIE
Scripture passages, favorite quotations, and charms illustrate the message of faith, hope, and love in this mini book. A stained glass–like inked window on the back page reveals a unique view of the cross charm, while additional embedded charms carry the theme from page to page.

SUPPLIES:

- 3″× 3″ Create & Treasure Ready-To-Go! Blank Board Book, black (C&T Publishing)

- Patterned papers: fleur rendezvous, palace rendezvous (Rusty Pickle); angel (Autumn Leaves); textured pearl (Provo Craft)

- Rub-ons: Scriptbooking *Faith* and *Love* (Decal Specialties)

- Stickers: Walk in Faith (Crossed Paths); Love Scripture verse 53C, 1 Corinthians 13 (It Takes Two); Faith, Mega vellum stickers (NRN Designs)

- "Faith," "Hope," and "Love" pewter cross charms (Crossed Paths); heart charms (Making Memories)

- Laser die cut word *Hope* (Sarah Heidt Photocraft)

- Ribbon, dancer (Offray)

- Spectrum clear acrylic square (Heidi Grace Designs)

- Alcohol inks: piñata, chili pepper red, calabaza orange, blanco blanco (Rupert, Gibbon & Spider)

- Craft knife

- Adhesive

- Thread

- Pen with black ink

- Circle punch

- ¹⁄₁₆″ hole punch

- Jump ring

INSTRUCTIONS:

1. For the front cover, cut a 3″ × 3″ piece of palace rendezvous patterned paper and tear a corner of textured pearl paper to fit the bottom right corner. Paste both to the cover. Next, attach the laser die cut *Hope* word and rub-on words *Faith* and *Love*; then attach a heart charm.

2. For the inside pages, cut a 3″ × 3″ square of fleur rendezvous paper for each page (do not affix yet).

3. Using the circle punch, make an opening for the "Hope" cross in the background paper and glue the paper onto the page. Next, using a craft knife, cut a window opening within the circle in the shape of the cross. The "Hope" cross will sit in a round silhouette hole so it will show on pages 4 and 5.

4. Dab alcohol inks, one color at a time, onto the clear acrylic square, allowing each color to dry before applying the next. Continue until the acrylic has a stained-glass appearance.

5. Using the acrylic square as your guide, cut window openings into pages 2 and 3 and the back cover. This is where the "Faith" cross and stained glass-like window will show through. Apply stickers and rub-ons.

6. For the back cover, cut a 3″ × 3″ square of textured pearl paper. Using the craft knife, cut a window opening from the paper for the stained glass-like window and paste paper onto the back cover

7. Dab adhesive onto the edges of the acrylic-inked window and position it into the opening on the back cover. Let dry. Glue on "Love" cross.

8. Punch a hole through the back cover with the 1/16″ hole punch. Attach the heart charm with a jump ring.

9. Thread a ribbon through the opening in the spine. Tie a second piece of ribbon to this one at the top of the spine. Tie smaller pieces of ribbon onto the second ribbon. When the spine is covered, tie the first and second ribbons together at the bottom of the spine. Trim.

10. Ink all exposed edges with the black pen.

J is for Jewelry

Joyful Season Mini-Book Necklace

BY LAURIE D'AMBROSIO

Share your joy in the season with this fun and easy-to-make mini Board Book necklace. Tuck in some of your favorite pictures with Santa and add a few mementos in the cutout niche. It's a perfect holiday-time accessory if you put in a favorite cookie recipe to give to a friend or to keep with you when you're grocery shopping so that you don't forget to pick up the right ingredients.

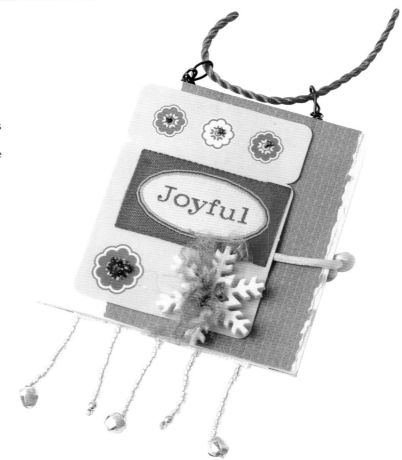

SUPPLIES:

- 3˝ × 3˝ Create & Treasure Ready-To-Go! Blank Board Book, white (C&T Publishing)
- Winter Sophisticates Paper Wardrobe Coordinates (Plaid)
- Deckle tear ruler (Plaid)
- Holiday charm and jingle bell fringe
- Seed beads
- Glue Dots
- Jewelry pliers and scissors (Tool-Tron)

- Aleene's Tacky Glue (Duncan)
- ⅛˝ punch
- Wooden mallet
- Cotton ball
- Wooden skewer
- Scissors
- Assorted snowflakes and confetti
- Green wire
- Green eyelets

- Green thread and fiber
- Green and red satin cord
- Micro-tip black marker
- Craft knife
- Clothespins

INSTRUCTIONS:

Cover

1. Use the deckle ruler to tear a 2¼″× 3″ strip from the red sweater or other patterned paper. Attach to the front cover with Glue Dots.

2. Stitch green and red seed beads into the centers of the flowers on the green paper die cut. Secure the threads with Glue Dots (do not knot).

3. Glue the "Joyful" label to the top of the die cut.

4. Use a piece of wire to thread fuzzy green fiber in the center of the snowflake embellishment. Glue to the die cut.

5. Cut a 6¼″ piece of light green satin cord. Place Glue Dots on each corner on the back of the die cut. Add glue where the cord will be located. Attach the die cut and satin cord tie to the front of the album and clamp with the clothespin until the glue dries.

Inside Pages

1. Using a craft knife, cut a 2″× 2″ window into the second-to-last page of the book.

2. Cut a strip of paisley or other decorative paper and glue to the facing page. Add monogram letter stickers to spell the word *Noel*.

3. Cut a piece of jingle bell trim and affix, using Glue Dots, to the bottom of the page. Be sure to fold the edge of the trim over, catching the tail. The thread tails must be secured or the beads will pull off.

4. Cut a 3″× 3″ piece of red chevron or other paper and paste to the second-to-last page with adhesive dots. Cut an X with the craft knife from the center of what will be the frame to each corner. Fold the flaps over the frame and secure with Glue Dots. Trim excess paper.

5. Cut a 3″× 3″ piece of green sweater or other paper. Glue to the last page of the book.

6. Cut a 6½″ piece of light green satin cord. Add adhesive to the four sides of the frame and sandwich the cord between the frame and the last page.

7. Use the hammer and punch to add holes to the top of the frame. Insert eyelets with adhesive and let dry.

8. Cut two 6″ pieces of wire. Thread them through the eyelets and fold in half. Pull one end over the skewer. Use jewelry pliers to wrap the wire, creating a loop. Pull and wrap the other end of the wire in the opposite direction to secure. Trim excess. Use the skewer to make sure that the book hangs level and the loops are even.

9. Thread the red twisted cord through the loops. Make an overhead knot and secure it with glue.

J is for Journaling

"I'm 28 for a Moment" Journal

BY CHRISTINA KIMMELL

This journaling concept came to me while hearing the "5 for Fighting" song. I wanted to document who I was and where I was at that point of my life. When I work on a small journal such as this, I choose a few products that I like and use them on every page in a different way, so that the album is tied together easily and flows from page to page. I used matte medium as my adhesive to achieve a seamless look, with no bubbles or lifting of the paper.

SUPPLIES:

- 6″× 6″ Create & Treasure Ready-To-Go! Blank Board Book, white heart (C&T Publishing)

- Cardstock, canary (Bazzill)

- Matte medium (Liquitex)

- Rub-on decals

- Postage stamp stickers (American Crafts, Pebbles Inc., Ma Vinci's Reliquary)

- Paintbrush

- Zig permanent marker

- ColorBox pigment brush pad, avocado (Clearsnap)

- Computer, printer, and paper for creating correctly sized photos

INSTRUCTIONS:

Cover

1. Cut canary cardstock to fit the heart shape of the cover and affix with matte medium.

2. Add rub-on decals and stickers to create the title. Use the permanent marker to write on any words that you don't have on hand.

3. Brush another layer of matte medium on top of everything for added protection.

4. Using the pigment brush pad, wipe color onto all the edges.

Inside Pages

1. Using a computer, resize and print out the desired photo on printer paper and cut it to the size and shape of the page. Apply with matte medium.

2. Hand-journal your story on the opposite page using a permanent marker. Add on any appropriate rub-ons or stickers that fit the theme.

3. Rub the pigment pad around all the edges.

K is for Keepsake

A Fairy-Tale Book

BY KATIE WATSON

This darling little book uses your children's photos to make a fairy-tale type of story. Children will love looking at the book and will delight in the idea of their pictures telling a little fairy tale! Complete with wings and fairy dust, it's a precious keepsake to cherish.

SUPPLIES:

- Patterned papers (My Mind's Eye, Chatterbox, Melissa Frances)
- Pink and white cardstock (Bazzill)
- Rickrack (Making Memories)
- Ribbon (Offray and American Crafts)
- Flower embellishments

- Letter stickers (American Crafts)
- Font, Fairy Princess (Two Peas in a Bucket)
- Glitter glue (Sulyn)
- Mono-Multi liquid glue (Tombow)
- White acrylic paint
- Chipboard

- Paintbrush
- Paper piercer or instant setter punch (Making Memories)
- Craft knife
- Decorative-edge scissors

INSTRUCTIONS:

Front Cover

1. Cover the front cover with gingham patterned paper using liquid glue.

2. Cut a square out of white cardstock that is ¼″ smaller than the gingham paper. Trim the edges using decorative-edge scissors and glue on top of the gingham paper. A small border of gingham paper should remain showing.

3. Cut another square out of the flower patterned paper about ¼″ smaller than the white cardstock from Step 2 and glue to the center of the white cardstock.

4. Turn the book so that the cover opens upward instead of sideways. Using letter stickers, make the title.

5. Thread gingham ribbon through the spine at the top of the book and tie in a bow, snipping off the ribbon edges at an angle.

Inside Pages

1. Apply layers of patterned papers and white cardstock using a similar method as for the cover.

2. Write out the first phrase of your story on white cardstock and paste it to the middle of the top page. Affix the first photo of your story to the bottom of the page. Design the remaining pages of the book in a similar fashion, adding to the story as you go.

3. Add small ribbons, rickrack, and flower embellishments to decorate the pages. Dab on some glitter glue to make them sparkle.

4. Using a paper piercer or punch, poke two holes all the way through to the front cover at the outer top edges of the book.

5. Thread a piece of translucent ribbon through two small artificial flowers, placed at each top corner, and tie in a knot. Snip the ends close to the knot. The knot should look like the center of the flower.

6. The ribbon that is coming out of the cover will act as the book closure, wrapped around the outside of the book and tied in a bow on the back cover.

Back Cover

1. Glue flower patterned paper across the entire back cover.

2. Cut two heart-shaped wings out of pink cardstock and paste gingham paper to the wings, trimming the paper to fit (set these aside).

3. Dry-brush the edges with white paint. Let dry.

4. Cut an oval shape for the top of the wing out of the gingham patterned paper and the same shape out of the chipboard. Glue the paper down on the chipboard.

5. Cut a smaller oval shape for the bottom of the wing out of the flower patterned paper and out of the chipboard. Glue the paper down on the chipboard.

6. Glue down the pieces of the top gingham wing so that they slightly overlap the bottom floral wing.

7. Dab glitter glue over the wings.

8. Poke holes in both wings for the brads to go through.

9. Put brads through the holes, attaching the wings to the back of the book.

10. Cover the back of the brad and the back of the wings with the pink cardstock covered in gingham paper.
Note: The wings will pivot to the back for storage.

L is for Leather

Luscious Leather Necklace

BY ARLINE LOWENTHAL

Leather is a luscious material that invites much experimentation, including the technique of intarsia. Intarsia is an inset process in which a cutout shape is replaced into a similar impressed shape, jigsaw puzzle–like. Provo Craft has provided the perfect tool to make intarsia simple, the Sizzix Paddle Punch.

SUPPLIES:

- 3″× 3″ Create & Treasure Ready-To-Go! Blank Board Book, black (C&T Publishing)

- Leather pieces (Tandy Leather Factory)

- Paper

- Sizzix Paddle Punch and small butterfly die (Provo Craft)

- Craft cutting mat

- Scissors

- Gold paint

- Paintbrush

- Gold paint pen (Krylon)

- Assorted rubber stamps

- Ink, bright colors and metallics

- Adhesive

- Plastic rhinestone jewels

- Ribbon

- Beaded necklace

INSTRUCTIONS:

1. Let's start with the butterflies. Decide on the color of leather you wish to use for the background of this page. I chose dark purple. Select the tiny butterfly die-cut shape and, using the craft mat underneath, cut a few butterflies out of paper. You will use the paper versions just to decide the placement of the butterflies on the page. Remember to leave room for the antennae.

2. Using another colorful piece of leather and assorted rubber stamps, stamp this piece of leather all over with various bright-colored inks, including metallic colors.

3. After the stamped leather is dry, move the butterfly die cut over the leather until you see a good place to make a very colorful butterfly. Then, working on the craft mat, take the hammer and hit the die cut a few times. Continue this process until you have cut out all the butterflies you want for the page.

4. Place the colorful leather butterflies on the piece of leather that will go into the book (using the positions you had decided on with your paper versions).

5. To make the intarsia spot, place the die cut exactly over the cutout butterflies. Carefully slip out the cutout butterflies, one at a time, and hammer out the die cut below.

6. Dab a bit of adhesive onto the butterfly and reposition it into the indented space you've just created on the piece of leather. Ease it into the leather until it is flush with the base leather. Continue this process until all the butterflies are where you planned for them to be.

7. Using the gold pen, draw in the antennae for each butterfly and glue a rhinestone at the end of each antenna.

8. Paint a gold border around the page to frame it and dab gold paint on the edges of the book as well to give it a cohesive look.

9. To turn your creation into a necklace, attach a ribbon closure and beaded string of your choice.

10. Decorate the cover with leather and a beaded creation to match.

 is for Mirror

Compact Mirror

BY PAM SESSIONS

Not your ordinary altered Board Book and not your ordinary compact mirror but a personalized combination of the two. Make an elegant compact for your mother or one that is funky and bright for a teenager. The inside cover can be decorated with a collage, a favorite quotation, or a photograph. Being small and thin, this compact mirror is the perfect size to slip into an evening bag for a night out.

SUPPLIES:

- 3″× 3″ Create & Treasure Ready-To-Go! Blank Board Book, white (C&T Publishing)
- Patterned paper: 12″× 12″, Romance Burnout (Junkitz)
- Ribbons: 38″ black sheer, 8″ black stitched grosgrain
- King's Buckle ribbon slide, silver (7Gypsies)

- Rub-ons: Rummage, black (Making Memories)
- 2″ square mirror (Darice)
- Snap
- Adhesives: Glue Dots, Glue Lines, Mod Podge (Plaid)
- Little girl image (ARTchix Studio)

- X-Acto knife
- Brayer
- Sewing needle
- Black thread
- Scissors

INSTRUCTIONS:

1. Cut 2 center pages out of the book, being careful not to damage the cover. Cut a 2″ square from the center of one page (this will be the frame for the mirror). Set the frame aside for later.

2. Cut a 4″×7¼″ piece of patterned paper for the cover. Score ½″ from each edge and in the center on the fold. Also score ¼″ on each side of the center fold and cut according to the drawing.

3. Using Mod Podge adhesive, wrap the cover with the patterned paper, securing the overlap to the inside cover. Using a brayer, roll out any air pockets and allow to dry. Apply a second coat of adhesive to the inside and outside covers.

4. Cut a 2¾″ square from patterned paper and paste it to the inside back cover. Add artwork, a quotation, or a photograph, using Mod Podge as necessary.

5. Cut off 1½″ of black stitched ribbon, tie into a bow, and set aside. Sew the two halves of a snap to the ends of a 6″ piece of the ribbon.

6. Thread the ribbon through the ribbon slide and glue to the cover with Glue Lines. Snap the book shut and paste the bow to the left of the snap.

7. Cut off 8″ of sheer black ribbon and set aside.

8. Using a 30″ piece of sheer black ribbon, wrap the frame, tightly securing the last corner with mini Glue Dots.

9. Cut the 8″ piece of sheer black ribbon into four 2″ pieces to wrap the corners. Secure with mini Glue Dots.

10. Insert the mirror into the frame and secure the frame to the inside front cover with Glue Dots or Glue Lines.

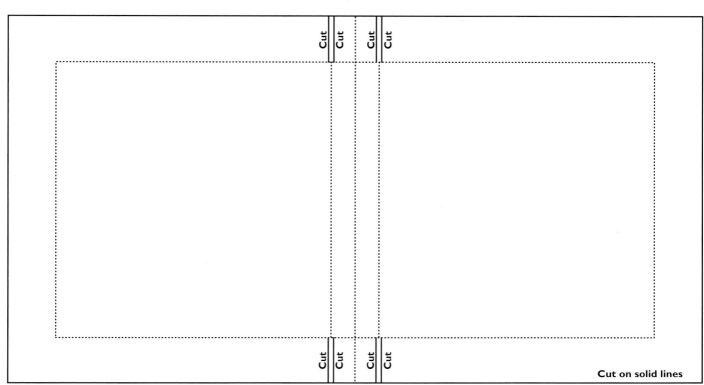

Cut on solid lines

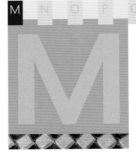

M is for Mosaic

Mosaic Pendant Necklace with Pocket

BY MADELINE ARENDT

I have developed an interest in altered book arts in the past few years and, with the wonderful products that manufacturers are producing, I've been able to challenge and stretch my imagination in creating some beautiful designs. For this project, my focus was to create something more than just a book. What I have come up with is this lovely piece of mosaic jewelry.

SUPPLIES:

- 3″ × 3″ Create & Treasure Ready-To-Go! Blank Board Book, black (C&T Publishing)
- Makin's Clay: black, natural
- Super Tape, sheet (Therm O Web)
- Inks: Posh Rainbow Precious Metals silver and rich gold; Tim Holtz Distress Ink, antique linen and black soot (Ranger)
- Super Fine Detail clear embossing powder (Ranger)
- Heat It! embossing tool (Ranger)
- Glossy Accents adhesive clear coating (Ranger)
- Inkssentials Memory Glass, 1½″ squares, 3 pieces (Ranger)
- Art Face stamp (Paula Best)
- Small fabric piece, approximately 9″× 6″

- Fabri-Tac glue (Beacon)
- Black elastic
- Small button
- Small piece of paper
- Crimp tool
- X-Acto knife
- Paper trimmer (optional)
- Paper awl
- Brush
- Pencil
- Acrylic roller
- Metal-edge ruler
- Jump rings
- Strand of beads for necklace

INSTRUCTIONS:

Making the Fabric Pocket

1. Using a ruler and knife, trim a thin strip ($\frac{1}{8}$″) away from the edge of the two center pages.

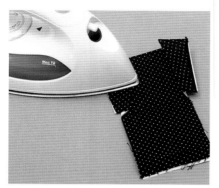

Making the gusseted fabric lining

2. Use the pattern on page 36 to cut the fabric lining. Make folds according to the pattern and press them in with an iron.

3. Using Fabri-Tac, glue the tiny hem at the top of the gusset. Glue the top fold over the edge of the first inner page.

4. Glue the edges of the gusset around the side edges of the second page.

5. Pierce holes at the top of both pages, centering them.

6. Thread a length of elastic to one side for a closure. Thread a button on a cord through the other. Knot or glue in place on the back side of each page to hold in place.

Working the Clay

1. Roll out the black clay, using an acrylic roller. Continue to roll until the clay is approximately $\frac{1}{16}$″ thick. Set the clay aside to air dry, following the package directions.

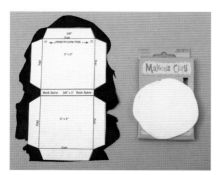

Each clay package makes enough for two pieces.

2. Roll out the natural-colored clay as in Step 1 until a thickness of approximately $\frac{1}{8}$″ is achieved. Set aside to dry.

3. Trace the clay cover template pattern from page 37 onto the dry black clay. Cut out using a ruler and X-Acto knife.

4. Trim the edges of natural clay evenly with a knife, making two square shapes approximately 3″ × 3″.

5. Dab metallic inks lightly with a dry brush onto the natural pieces of clay and allow to dry.

6. Cut the painted clay pieces into mosaic squares with a ruler and knife, or use a paper trimmer. The pieces should be approximately $\frac{3}{8}$″ square.

Covering the Book with Clay

1. Use the pattern on page 37 to cut the pieces from the Super Tape. Glue the flaps of clay over the edges of the front and back covers. Clamp with binder clips until the glue dries completely.

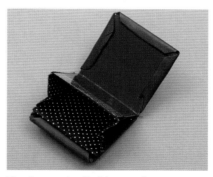

The clay remains flexible enough to wrap around the cover.

> **NOTE**
>
> *Before applying the black clay to the outside covers, test the fit by placing it on the book and folding the edges over. Make any necessary changes before applying the clay and tape to the book.*

2. Using a paper awl, pierce a hole in each corner and insert a jump ring (this is where you will attach a beaded necklace of your choice).

Adding the Mosaic Pattern

1. Apply a $2\frac{1}{2}$″ square of tape to the center of the outside cover. Remove the backing paper.

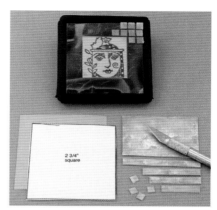

Apply mosaic pieces, spacing them as evenly as possible.

2. Using tweezers, set the tiny mosaic pieces onto the tape in any desired pattern.

3. When all the mosaic pieces are in place, coat the entire cover with Glossy Accents. Begin with a bead around the outside edge of the mosaic pieces, working the liquid along the spaces between and over the tiny squares.

4. Set aside until dry. Reapply Glossy Accents if necessary.

Adding Glass-Covered Faces
(Optional)

Stamped images covered with glass are an added embellishment to the covers.

1. On a small piece of paper, stamp the desired image, using the black soot ink. Apply clear embossing powder to the ink. Pour off excess powder. Heat with a heat tool to emboss.

2. Lay a glass square onto the image, centering it. Mark the placement and trim. Place a small dot of Glossy Accents on each corner of the paper and then place the glass over the image to affix both pieces.

3. Center the glass-covered face (one on each cover) by placing it over the mosaic pieces. Add a small scrap of tape to hold it in place.

> **NOTE**
>
> *When Glossy Accents is applied over everything on the cover and left to dry, the square will be held in place.*

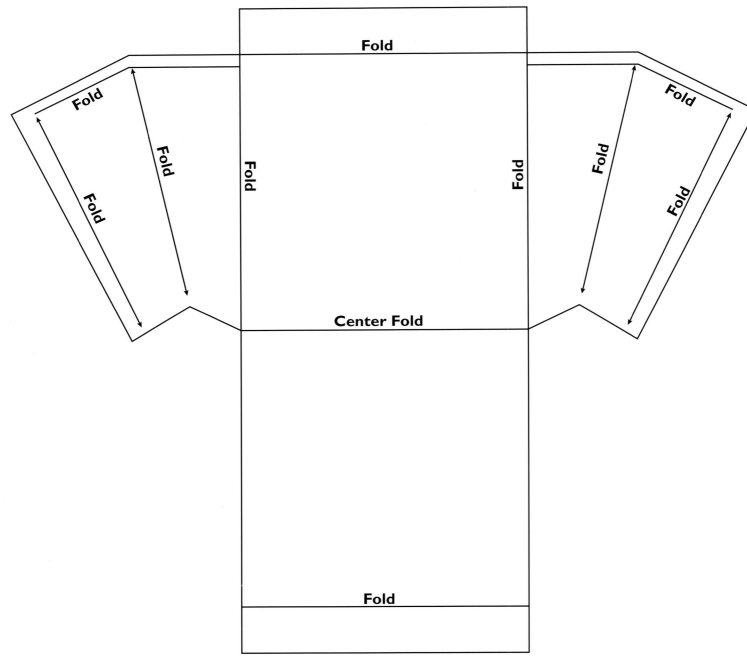

Fabric Lining Pattern: Press all folds into fabric before gluing and attaching to book.

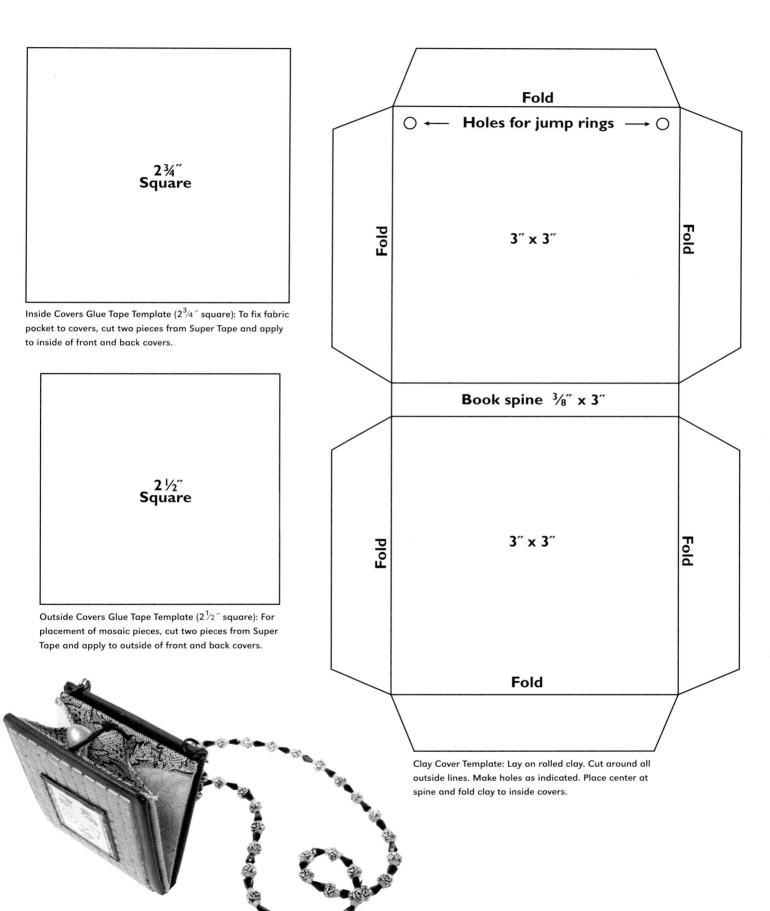

**2¾″
Square**

Inside Covers Glue Tape Template (2¾″ square): To fix fabric pocket to covers, cut two pieces from Super Tape and apply to inside of front and back covers.

**2½″
Square**

Outside Covers Glue Tape Template (2½″ square): For placement of mosaic pieces, cut two pieces from Super Tape and apply to outside of front and back covers.

Fold

○ ← **Holes for jump rings** → ○

Fold

3″ x 3″

Fold

Book spine ⅜″ x 3″

Fold

3″ x 3″

Fold

Fold

Clay Cover Template: Lay on rolled clay. Cut around all outside lines. Make holes as indicated. Place center at spine and fold clay to inside covers.

N is for Niche

A Treasure Box of Memories

BY ANGELA DANIELS

My little boy is four years old and completely preoccupied with studying the ground as we take walks. He can spot a shimmering object from yards away and wants to take everything home, including small bits of tin, broken buttons, and tiny pebbles. I made this mini treasure-box book with him in mind. I thought that he could hang it from his backpack and put the little "treasures" that he found inside the built-in niche. I figured this would help keep the items collected down to a smaller size and give him somewhere special to keep what he finds.

SUPPLIES:

- 3″ × 3″ Create & Treasure Ready-To-Go! Blank Board Book, white (C&T Publications)

- Patterned papers: 12″ × 12″, Playful Wide Rule, Playful Palette, Playful Petite Pop (KI Memories)

- Playful Wisdom Wise Words die cuts (KI Memories)

- Salsa Script Expressionz rub-ons (Junkitz)

- Photo of child

- Household twine, red

- Button

- Mini Glue Dots (Stampin' Up!)

- Clear tape

- Adhesive, mixed media

- Large square punch (Stampin' Up!)

- Small acrylic bead box

- Pencil

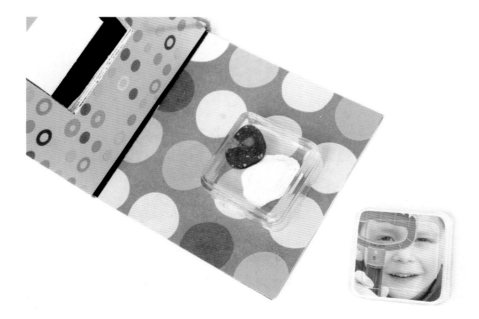

When I grow up I want to be a little boy.

–Joseph Heller

INSTRUCTIONS:

1. Trace the front and back covers of the Board Book onto a piece of Playful Wide Rule patterned paper and then cut the sheet large enough to cover the entire outside of the book. Apply using a mixed-media glue.

2. Using rub-on letters, spell the title on the front cover.

3. Tie a piece of twine through the button and paste to the front cover with a Glue Dot.

4. Run another piece of the twine through the spine of the book and tie it at the top to give the spine some interest and dimension.

5. Using a large square punch, punch a square opening through the paper-covered front cover. Be sure that the window you punch will be large enough for the acrylic box to fit through.

6. After covering the inside pages with other decorative papers, punch square openings into the two middle pages. Glue these two pages together to create dimension inside the book. There is no need to cover the pages that will be glued together.

7. Add a small quotation to the first page, applying it with mixed-media glue.

8. Using a small piece of clear tape, affix the small photo of child to the inside lid of the acrylic box.

9. To affix the acrylic box to the book, attach small slices of Glue Dots to the bottom edge of the acrylic box (covering as much of the edge as you can for stability) and then position the box and press firmly to make it stick. The book should open and close easily. The acrylic box will fit through the windows that you have cut into the cover and inside pages.

10. Fill the niche you've created with small treasures.

O is for Ornament

"Merry Christmas" Ornament

BY DENA COE

This project teaches you how to turn an ordinary Board Book into an extraordinary Christmas tree ornament. Using a mixture of patterned papers, ribbons, and embellishments, you can create an amazing work of art that is a perfect gift or a wonderful keepsake for your own tree.

SUPPLIES:

- 3″× 3″ Create & Treasure Ready-To-Go! Blank Board Book, black (C&T Publishing)

- Patterned papers: watermelon, black-eyed peas, weathered thyme, weathered white, and weathered black (Lasting Impressions)

- Christmas sticker sheets: Season's Cheer, Joy (Penny Black)

- Doodads: Tim Holtz Print Blocks, Typewriter (Design Originals)

- Brads, 6, black (Making Memories)

- Loopy brads, 2, copper (Karen Foster Design)

- ColorBox ink, charcoal (Clearsnap)

- Ribbon: four 12″ pieces and one 24″ piece, assorted colors and styles

- Glitter gel, Icicle Stickles (Ranger)

- Foam Dots, Pop Dots (Therm O Web)

- Sanding block (Making Memories)

- Computer fonts, assorted

- Embossing powder, clear

- Heat embossing tool (Marvy Uchida)

- Watermark ink pad, VersaMark (Tsukineko)

- Ultimate! adhesive (Crafter's Pick)

- Universal hole punch (Making Memories)

INSTRUCTIONS:

Cover

1. Cut a 3″× 3″ square of watermelon paper and sand the edges using a sanding block. Paste to the front cover of the book and trim any excess.

2. Cut letters to form the word *Merry* from the Print Blocks doodads and cut the letters for *Christmas* from the Typewriter doodads.

3. Ink the edges of the *M, E, R, R,* and *Y* letters with black ink. When dry, stamp with the watermark ink pad and dip the letters into clear embossing powder. Using the heat tool, heat until the powder has melted.

4. Cut the ornament sticker from the sheet of stickers (do not peel off the backing at this time) and trace the outside edge of the ornament with glitter gel. Allow to dry and affix the sticker to the center of the cover, allowing room for the words above and below it.

5. Add the words *Merry* and *Christmas* to the book as shown.

6. For the spine, trim a piece of weathered thyme paper to 1″ and score it in the middle to accommodate the spine, approximately ³⁄8″. Sand the edges and affix it to the front and back covers, using adhesive.

7. To attach the clasp, set even holes approximately ³⁄16″ for the loopy brads on the front and back covers. Insert and close the brads. *Note: Do this step before pasting paper to the inside pages of the book, so that you cover up the brad clasps.*

8. String a 24″ length of green and gold ribbon through the clasps and tie together.

Inside Pages

1. Cut 3″× 3″ squares of black-eyed peas and weathered thyme papers, sand edges, and paste one piece to each page. Trim any excess paper.

2. Mount a gift sticker onto a piece of 2³⁄4″ × 2³⁄4″ weathered black paper and sand the edges of the paper.

3. Attach a 4″ piece of ribbon to the mounted sticker, approximately ¹⁄8″ from the top edge of the sticker. Make a small hole through the ribbon and sticker and insert a brad. Affix it to the page using Pop Dots for a three-dimensional look.

4. Cut and sand a piece of 2³⁄4″ × 2¹⁄4″ weathered white paper. Print the desired phrase and attach a 4″ piece of ribbon as in Step 3 above. Affix to the page using adhesive.

 **P** is for Painting

Once Upon a Time

BY DEBRA COOPER

Board Books are usually made for the enjoyment of children. In this case, with a little painting and decorating, they're just as much fun for the adult to create. We cannot promise a child a perfect world, but we can try to deliver a pretend one for her through a custom-designed book starring that special little someone in our lives. In this unique book, the child is portrayed in a wonderful and fanciful world created for her, which includes all her favorite things: flowers, butterflies, birds, and home. What child wouldn't want to star in her own storybook?

SUPPLIES:

- 6″ × 6″ Create & Treasure Ready-To-Go! Blank Board Book, white, accordion (C&T Publishing)

- Acrylic craft paint: FolkArt Cayman blue, Hauser green light (Plaid)

- Permopaque pigment markers: white, red (Sakura)

- Glitter glue: Ice Stickles gold ice (Ranger)

- Tim Holtz Distress Ink, black soot (Ranger)

- Permanent black marker

- Buttons: Foofala Bag O Buttons summer collection (Autumn Leaves)

- Patterned papers: Foofala Thrify Words Thrift Store collection, Bandana Summer collection (Autumn Leaves)

- Flower and bird clip-art images: The Big Box of Art (Hemera Technologies)

- Black-and-white photocopies or inkjet prints of children's photographs

- Hand-drawn stencil in the shape of a tree, house, etcetera, on cardstock or manila folder

- Adhesive

- Paintbrushes, assorted sizes

- Rickrack

INSTRUCTIONS:

1. Determine where the front of the book will be. The accordion should open from the right side of the book.

2. Paint the top three-quarters of all the pages of the book with blue paint and allow it to dry to the touch. Make sure the paint covers all the edges of the book.

3. Along the bottom of the book, paint light green in a wavy pattern until it slightly overlaps the blue paint.

4. Add some clouds using the opaque white marker, and apply a bit of glitter glue along edges of each cloud.

5. While the book is drying, draw the outline of a tree and a house onto cardstock or a manila folder and cut out. By creating a stencil, you can use the template over again in your future projects.

6. Cut trees from the Thrifty Words patterned paper and adhere to the cover and inside pages as you like. Affix assorted buttons to the branches. Cut the house from the Bandana patterned paper and glue to an inside page; paste a bird on the roof as an added fun touch.

7. Affix two 12″ pieces of red rickrack along the top and bottom of the cover. They should wrap around the front and back covers.

8. Crop out photos of the children who will be starring in the story and paste them along the bottom of the cover and inside pages.

9. Clip and apply birds and butterflies and affix as if they were flying across the sky. Use the red opaque marker to draw a heart in a bird's mouth or color in a butterfly's wings. Add some clipped flowers along the ground and add color to them as well if you like.

10. Using black ink or permanent marker, write the title and words to your story.

P is for Personalized

"Chase the Blues Away" Book

BY STEFANIE OLBRICH

I created this personalized mini Board Book for my son Ben's first day of school, as a way for him to chase the lonely blues away and be reminded of home. In it, I included photos of close family members (parents, sister, and grandparents), pieces of fabric, a picture of his lovey—a favorite stuffed animal—and treasures (found objects) that he had collected at home. With this book, I wanted to remind him of how close we all really are even if he feels he is alone at school. I included journaling on almost every page of the book to reinforce our love for him.

SUPPLIES:

- 3″ × 3″ Create & Treasure Ready-To-Go! Blank Board Book, black (C&T Publishing)

- 8½″ × 11″ cardstock, blue monochromatic (Bazzill)

- Problem Secretary font (Scrap Village)

- Blue slide mount (Loersch)

- Ribbon: 12″ length each, white and black (Offray)

- Silver 1¼″ keychain ring (Hillman)

- Patterned papers: 3″ × 3″ pieces, blue stripes (Laura Ashley, EK Success); clouds (Current)

- Alligator clip, silver (optional)

- Decorative brad (Making Memories)

- X-Acto knife

- Pens: Sharpie extra fine point, blue (Sanford); Permaball medium point, black (Pilot)

- Adhesives: Mini Glue Dots; double-sided tape (Pioneer); foam tape (3M)

- Tim Holtz Distress Ink, walnut (Ranger)

- Spray bottle with water

- Iron

- Paper punch or awl

Benjamin, today you start school, big boy school, for the first time ever. We are all so very proud of you, but we know that this transition is difficult. I have created this book for you to keep on your school bag, as a reminder of us, as a reminder of home, and as a reminder that we will be waiting for you every day after school. We all love you tons, and want you to know that we are never far. If you get lonely or home sick just pull out this book and look at our pictures, or touch Sheepie, or look at your treasures and remember that we love you. And know that you will succeed! ♡ mama

Unclip and flip up for more photos

INSTRUCTIONS:

Cover

1. Cut a 3″× 3″ piece of blue cardstock to fit the front cover. Print the book title on cardstock with the Problem Secretary font.

2. Paste a small family photo to the back of a slide mount.

3. Knot white pieces of ribbon in the corners of the slide mount.

4. Affix the slide mount to the cardstock with foam tape.

5. Paste the cardstock to the book cover with Glue Dots.

Inside Pages

1. Cut a 3″× 3″ piece of blue striped patterned paper. Age paper by first crumpling it and then flattening it out again. Next, rub distress ink into the creases and spray the paper with water. Finally, iron the paper to dry and smooth it out.

2. Computer generate your journaling using the same font as on the cover and print it out onto the distressed paper created in Step 1. Add a handwritten sentiment at the bottom with permanent ink.

3. Paste the journaled paper to the first page using double-sided tape.

4. For the photo page, gather about five photos to be used in the album and trim all to the same size (approximately 2¼″ × 2¾″). Label the back of each photo with the person's name and the date on which the photo was taken, using permanent ink.

5. Punch a hole in the top left corner of each photo. Punch a hole in the book page where the photos will be positioned.

6. Paste a 3″× 3″ piece of cloud patterned paper to the book page. Slide a decorative brad through the holes in the photos and then through the patterned paper and book. Secure the brad on the back of the page by bending the prongs back. The photos should now swivel on the brad.

7. Flip the photos up and write a hidden sentiment underneath the last photo, using permanent ink.

8. Optional: Add a silver alligator clip to hold the photos together. Type out and affix, below the photos, instructions to flip the pictures up.

9. Continue journaling and adding items of sentiment throughout the remaining pages of the book. Some items to consider adding are pieces of fabric or a photo of a favorite stuffed animal as well as leaves, shells, or other items from a collection.

10. Finish the project by running a 12″ length of black ribbon through the space created in the spine of the book when the book is open. Tie the ribbon into a knot at the top of the spine. Loop a keychain ring through one of the ends of the ribbon, and then tie the ribbon into a knot again at the top of the ribbon to secure the keychain ring. This can be used to hang the book from a backpack.

Q is for Quotations

Goddess Magic

BY LEA CIOCI

Quotations are a fast and easy way to express thoughts and feelings. They are a charming way to personalize your art by quickly conveying a theme or the symbolism represented in the images you use. Quotations add inspiration and uniqueness to your project. For a touch of merriment, include bright colors—they will reflect the ambiance of the art you are creating. Feel free to express yourself through your art!

SUPPLIES:

- 3″ x 3″ Create & Treasure Ready-To-Go! Blank Board Book, white (C&T Publishing)

- Sea Bright inks: citrus, pool, purple surf (Ranger)

- Twinkling H20s: key lime, passion, mystic blue, sunburst, golden opal (LuminArte)

- Hearty clay (Mountain Idea)

- Sun/moon art mould (Krafty Lady)

- Night goddess art stamp (After Midnight)

- Adhesive-backed vellum (Vintage Workshop)

- Computer paper

- Computer with scanner

- Adhesive-backed Velcro circles

- Rectangle of purple suede leather

- E6000 glue

- Awl or Japanese screw punch

- Circle jump ring (Junkitz)

- Premade necklace

- Scissors

- Glitter glue

- Memory Tape Runner (Therm O Web)

- Small, flat watercolor brush

INSTRUCTIONS:

Cover

1. Bright-colored inks heavily dragged across the surface of the book add the base color to the cover. Start with the citrus color and drag the ink pad over the top third of the book. Next, use the pool color and drag the edge of the ink pad over the center. Using the edge of the ink pad allows you to put just a small area of ink where you want it. Last, drag the purple on the bottom third of the page and let dry.

2. To add shimmer and further color, paint Twinkling H20s lightly over the inks using a watercolor brush.

3. Add words by creating them on a computer and printing them out on adhesive-backed vellum. Remove the backing from the words and press them into place.

4. To create the sun/moon clay accent, form a small ball-sized piece of Hearty clay and press it into the mould. Remove the clay from the mould, let dry, and then paint with Twinkling H20s. Affix the clay accent to the book cover using E6000 glue.

5. Using the Japanese screw punch, create the hole for the jump ring by punching through the top left corner of the book. It will take two to three punches to get through all the pages. Place the jump ring through the hole and attach the premade necklace.

6. To attach the leather book closure, press a Velcro loop circle to the front open edge of the book and a Velcro hook circle to one end of the rectangular piece of suede. Connect the hooks and loops together, then bring the opposite end of the suede rectangle to the back of the book and glue in place with E6000 glue.

Inside Pages

1. Following Step 1 for the cover, use citrus ink and drag it over the surface. Paint key lime Twinkling H20s over the top.

2. Using your computer, scan a stamped image of the night goddess and shrink the size down to fit on a 3″ × 3″ page. Print out the image and the Shakti Gawain quote on regular computer paper. Paint the image and the quote with Twinkling H20s. Let dry. Affix the quotation and image using Memory Tape Runner.

3. Edge the quotation with a light bead of glitter glue and add dots on the page with additional glitter glue spots. Let dry.

4. Create the Julia Cameron quote, stars, and little swirls on your computer and print them out on adhesive-backed vellum. Cut them out, remove the backing, and press into place. Accent the vellum stars and swirls by painting Twinkling H20s over them.

R is for Recipe Book

Recipe Book with Cookie Mix

BY KATIE WATSON

For some gift-giving magic, turn a Board Book into an old-fashioned recipe book. Add it to a simple mason jar filled with cookie-making ingredients and you have created a true delight. The book, combined with the jar of delicious cookie mix, makes a great gift or a creative fund-raiser idea.

1 CUP ALL-PURPOSE FLOUR
1 TEASPOON GROUND CINNAMON
1/2 TEASPOON GROUND NUTMEG
1 TEASPOON BAKING SODA
1/2 TEASPOON SALT
3/4 CUP RAISINS
2 CUPS ROLLED OATS
3/4 CUP PACKED BROWN SUGAR
1/2 CUP WHITE SUGAR

OATMEAL RAISIN SPICE COOKIES

SUPPLIES:

- 3″ × 3″ Create & Treasure Ready-To-Go! Blank Board Book, white (C&T Publishing)

- Cooking stickers and die cuts (EK Success, Creative Imaginations)

- Cardstock (Bazzill)

- Patterned paper: wild asparagus, floral, gingham, striped (My Mind's Eye, Daisy D's)

- Vintage line (Making Memories)

- Rickrack (Making Memories)

- Ribbon (American Crafts)

- Font: Little Days (downloaded off Internet)

- Ultimate! adhesive (Crafter's Pick)

- Glue Dots

- Pinking shears

- Lightweight cloth

- Mason jar with screw-top lid

INSTRUCTIONS:

Front Cover

1. Paste floral patterned paper to cover the front of the book.

2. Paste a strip of gingham patterned paper across the bottom of the cover.

3. Glue a piece of rickrack on the line where the two patterned papers meet.

4. Print the title of the recipe on white cardstock and cut each word out into a word strip.

5. Mat each word strip to a piece of striped patterned paper. Trace the outline of each word strip with a thin marker to make it stand out.

Inside Pages

1. Glue down the striped patterned paper to cover the pages, leaving a thin border of white all the way around each page.

2. Print out the recipe directions and cut them into word strips.

3. Mat the word strips on solid-colored cardstock or coordinating patterned paper.

4. Glue the word strips down in the order of the recipe.

5. Fill in blank spaces with cooking embellishments.

6. Thread ribbon through the spine of the book and tie in a double knot on the front cover. Snip the ribbon edges at an angle.

Recipe Jar

1. Layer ingredients in a quart-sized canning jar.

2. Cut lightweight cloth in a circle using pinking shears.

3. Cover the top of the jar with the cloth by putting the cloth circle underneath the screw top of the jar.

4. Tie a ribbon around the jar lid, securing it with Glue Dots. Tie a bow in front.

5. Hang tags with cooking embellishments, mini cookie cutters, or mini cooking utensils from the ribbon.

6. Make a label for the front of the jar out of scraps and glue it to the front of the jar using liquid glue. Be sure not to cover too much of the jar—you want to be able to see the layers of ingredients.

Oatmeal Raisin Spice Cookie Recipe

BY LISA, WITH PERMISSION FROM
WWW.ALLRECIPES.COM

INGREDIENTS

- 1 cup all-purpose flour
- 1 teaspoon ground cinnamon
- ½ teaspoon ground nutmeg
- 1 teaspoon baking soda
- ½ teaspoon salt
- ¾ cup raisins
- 2 cups rolled oats
- ¾ cup packed brown sugar
- ½ cup white sugar
- ¾ cup butter or margarine, softened
- 1 egg, slightly beaten
- 1 teaspoon vanilla

NOTE:

The butter, egg and vanilla will not be added to the jar of dry ingredients.

DIRECTIONS

1. Mix together flour, ground cinnamon, ground nutmeg, baking soda, and salt. Set aside.

2. Layer ingredients in the following order into a 1-quart widemouthed canning jar: flour mixture, raisins, rolled oats, brown sugar, and white sugar. It will be a tight fit; be sure to pack down each layer firmly before adding the next.

3. Attach the recipe book with the following instructions:

To Make Oatmeal Raisin Spice Cookies

1. Preheat oven to 350°F (175°C). Line cookie sheets with parchment paper.

2. Empty jar of cookie mix into large mixing bowl. Use your hands to mix thoroughly.

3. Mix in butter or margarine. Stir in egg and vanilla. Mix until completely blended. You will need to finish mixing with your hands. Shape into balls the size of walnuts. Place on a parchment-lined cookie sheet 2″ apart.

4. Bake for 11 to 13 minutes, or until edges are lightly browned. Cool for 5 minutes on cookie sheet. Transfer cookies to wire racks to finish cooling.

S is for Soft Sculpture

"Pull Yourself Together" Doll

BY ELINOR PEACE BAILEY

There is nothing more fun than blending the worlds of fabric and paper. For this project, I used a pin face, a stuffed square, a couple of yo-yos, and some charms from Artgirlz and joined them all together to create this book. I put the head on the front and the butt on the back. In between is the story of pulling myself together

SUPPLIES:

- 3″ x 3″ Create & Treasure Ready-To-Go! Blank Board Book, white (C&T Publishing)
- Sewing machine (Bernina)
- Scraps of fabric
- Button and craft thread (Coats & Clark)
- #7-gauge long darner (John James)
- Small amount of Poly-fil (Fairfield)
- Tacky glue
- Permawriter II .03, brown (Y&C)
- Brush-tipped permanent marking pens (Fabricmate)
- Colored pencils
- Arm and leg charms (Artgirlz)

INSTRUCTIONS:

1. Using the pin doll face pattern on page 52, cut out the face from a flesh-colored fabric scrap.

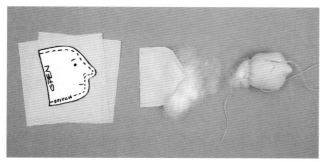

Creating the pin doll's face

2. Stitch the profile, leaving the flat side open. Clip and turn.

3. Using the long darner and a knotted thread, gather around the raw edge, stuff with Poly-fil, and cinch in the gathers. Tie them off and bring your needle to where the eyes should be and exit. Reenter at the same spot, a few threads away, and repeat, going back and forth until the indentation holds. Tie off with a colonial knot and bury the thread.

Making the collar

4. Cut two 3˝ squares for the doll's collar from a selected scrap of fabric. With right sides together and a ⅛˝ seam, stitch around the square. Slash at the middle of the back. Turn the square from the slash and lightly stuff the square. Use a ladder stitch to attach the head to the square. Copy the face on the template to the face of the pin doll using a fine-tipped permanent marking pen and fabric brush-tipped marking pens. Use colored pencils to rouge the cheeks.

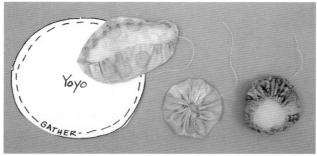

Making a yo-yo

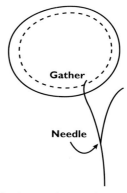

Sewing a gather into the yo-yo

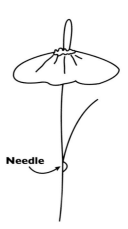

Pulling together the yo-yo

Finished yo-yo

5. To make the back end of the doll, use the pattern of the yo-yo and cut out two pieces, one for the dress and one for the panties or bottom. Using a knotted thread and the long darner, gather around the circles by hand. Stuff one with Poly-fil and leave the other flat.

6. Cinch in the gathers and stick the needle through the center of the gathers to the other side and pull.

Assembling the back end of the book

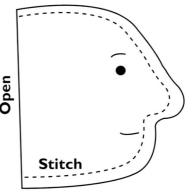

Pin doll's face pattern

Open

Stitch

7. Join the stuffed yo-yo to the flat one, with the pleats facing each other. From the center of the stuffed yo-yo, bring a thread under the stuffed yo-yo to form a butt. Tie off and bury the thread.

8. Stitch on the arm charms under the collar. Glue this unit to the front of the book. Add the leg charms under the bottom. Glue this unit to the back of the book. What you put in the middle of the book should explain your need to pull yourself together.

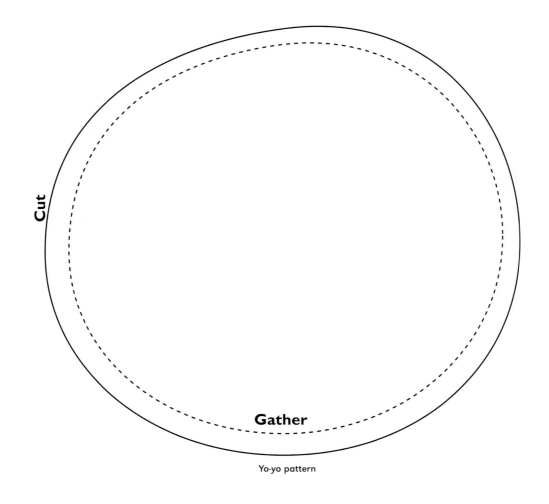

Cut

Gather

Yo-yo pattern

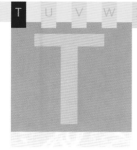

T is for Transformation

Emergency Purse

BY KAREN DESMET

This cute mini purse, made from a transformed Board Book, makes a perfect little gift for an overnight house guest, a bride, a bridesmaid, or your best friend. In addition to the handy compact mirror tucked inside, there are little envelopes containing lip ointment, an emergency sewing kit, headache medicine, spare change, and mini nail files.

SUPPLIES:

- 3″× 3″ Create & Treasure Ready-To-Go! Blank Board Book, white (C&T Publishing)
- Patterned papers: pink, floral (Anna Griffin)
- Fleece Finished fringe, 6″ (Trimtex)
- One strand bulk beads
- Button with adhesive
- Velcro closure dot
- Mod Podge (Plaid)
- Super Tape, ½″ (Therm O Web)

- Packaging tape (3M)
- String tags
- Mirror, 2″ square (Darice)
- Black paint
- Diamond Glaze (JudiKins)
- Ribbon
- Brads
- Small envelopes, plastic or vellum
- X-Acto knife

- Travel-size items such as sewing kit, nail files, lip ointment, etcetera (travel section of grocery store)
- Additional 3″× 3″ white Board Book or chipboard of same thickness
- Small piece of old sewing pattern
- Paintbrush
- Paper piercer
- Needle threader

INSTRUCTIONS:

Preparing the Book

1. Cut four 1″× 3″× 3″ triangles from the additional Board Book (or chipboard of same thickness). These will be used for the sides of the cover to create the purse shape.

2. Using wide single-sided packaging tape, attach the triangles to the sides of the book covers. Be sure to use tape on both sides of the triangle for added strength.

3. Keeping the book closed, brush Mod Podge on the front. Place pink patterned paper over the adhesive, then flip the book over and do the same on the back of the book. Once the cover is dry, trim the paper to the edge of the book.

4. Open the book to the middle section and pierce two holes in the spine's crease. These holes will help secure the beaded handle.

5. Put the wire from a needle threader through the pierced holes and pull the ends of the bead string through to form the beaded handle. Secure the strings with tape.

6. Open the book and cover the inside pages with pink patterned paper, using Mod Podge as in Step 3, and let dry.

7. Cut two 3″ pieces of fringe trim and paste one to each cover with Super Tape as shown.

Inside Pages

1. Create a chipboard frame that will fit around the mirror. Paint the frame black. When dry, sand the edges and use Diamond Glaze to seal. Glue frame and mirror to inside cover. Apply the rub-on words *Look Here*.

2. For the facing page, cut two 2½″ squares out of floral patterned paper. Adhere one square. Tear a ½″ strip from the top of the second square and fold up the bottom edge to form a pocket. Decorate, using brads and a piece of ribbon. Add a tag with the words *Lip Service* and fill the pocket with lip ointment packets.

3. For the sewing kit page, adhere a small piece of an old sewing pattern to the page. Put a little sewing kit in a small clear bag and attach the bag to the page.

4. On the facing page, using an envelope big enough to hold an aspirin packet, tie a piece of ribbon around the package, and add a "Head Help" tag. Insert medicine into packet and affix to page.

5. Continue adding mini envelopes to the remaining pages and fill them with helpful travel-sized items. Add tags to identify contents.

Closure

1. Cut a strip of chipboard that will fit from the back of the book to the front.
Note: The length will vary depending on how bulky the book becomes due to the contents of the envelopes inside.

2. Cover the chipboard in pink patterned paper and affix to the back.

3. Fold the board around until it reaches the front.

4. Attach a Velcro dot for the closure and a big white button for embellishment.

U is for Unique Shapes

Angled Photo Pendant

BY DEBORAH MACPHERSON

This is a charming little brag book with the pages cut into unique shapes. Wear it as necklace or hang it from your tree as an ornament. Put pictures of your children or grandchildren inside and you'll always have them close to your heart and ready to show off. The beaded fastener is designed to stay on even when you're looking at the photos.

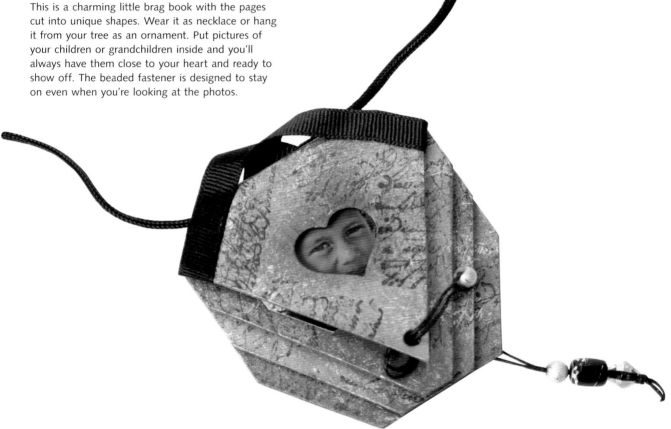

SUPPLIES:

- 3″ x 3″ Create & Treasure Ready-To-Go! Blank Board Book, black (C&T Publishing)

- Paper templates (provided)

- Pencil

- Craft or utility knife

- Cutting mat

- Sizzix Paddle Punch, heart shape

- ⅛″ hole punch

- Acrylic paints: Lumiere violet gold, metallic gold, pearl blue (Jacquard)

- Paintbrushes or sponges

- Silver leafing pen ink (Krylon)

- Scruffy brush

- Ink pad, StazOn jet black (Tsukineko)

- Rubber stamp, Illuminata (Inkadinkado)

- Waxed linen, Mainstays, 16″, black (Sulyn)

- Glass and metal beads, assorted

- Two 4″ pieces ⅜″ black grosgrain ribbon (Offray)

- Wonder Tape, ½″ (Suze Weinburg)

- Black craft cord, Needloft, 33″ (Uniek)

INSTRUCTIONS:

1. Using the templates, mark the cutting lines on the book pages.

2. Sliding the cutting mat between pages as needed, cut the pages into the unique shapes.

3. Slide the cutting mat between the first and second pages and punch a heart-shaped opening in the center with the Sizzix Paddle Punch.

4. Punch a $1/8''$ hole near the bottom of each page (the holes should align).

5. Paint the entire Board Book with Lumiere paints, being sure to paint the outer and inner edges of the punched holes. Let the book dry for 24 hours.

6. To use the ink from the silver leafing pen, tap the tip of the pen onto a paper plate to make a small puddle of paint; working quickly, dip the ends of a scruffy brush into the paint and lightly dab it onto the book.

7. Stamp randomly over the entire surface, using the black ink pad and the Illuminata rubber stamp.

8. Thread a round silver bead onto one end of the 16″ piece of black waxed linen, leaving it halfway down the waxed linen. Double the waxed linen and thread both ends into the front hole of the book. Once you've pulled the string through all the pages, thread some additional beads onto the waxed linen and knot it at the end. The round silver bead should end up on the top cover and the remaining beads on the bottom, acting as a pull cord that closes the pages of the book.

9. Wrap a 4″ piece of black grosgrain ribbon around the left front edge of the cover, using Wonder Tape to hold it in place on the back of the page. Loop ribbon over the top of the book and tape it onto the back, turning under $1/2''$. Repeat with another 4″ piece of ribbon on the right edge, crossing the ribbons at the top and securing them on the back.

10. Thread the 33″ piece of black craft cord through the ribbon and tie into a knot to make a necklace.

11. Insert photos of your favorite kids to complete this simple little brag book.

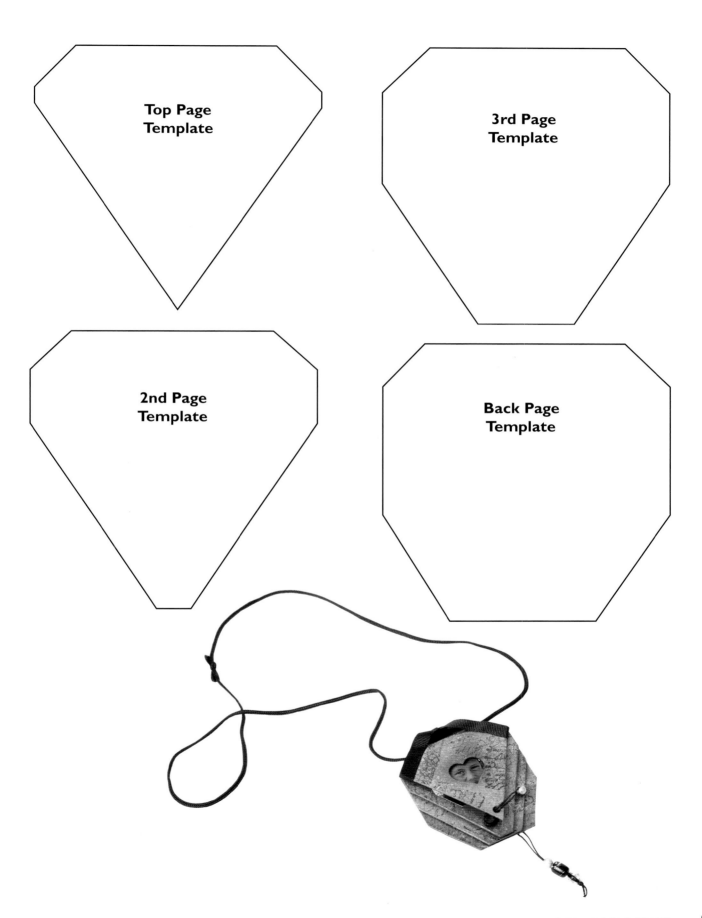

**Top Page
Template**

**3rd Page
Template**

**2nd Page
Template**

**Back Page
Template**

V is for Variations

"Sunny-Side Up" Necklace

BY SHARON MANN

This creative little necklace book provides many variations on the sun theme and is the perfect addition to your eclectic jewelry collection. It's easy to make with simple beading, collage, colored pencil, and watercolor techniques. Your friends will all want to make the Sunny-Side Up necklace when they see you wear it to your next book club meeting.

SUPPLIES:

- 3"× 3" Create & Treasure Ready-To-Go! Blank Board Book, black (C&T Publishing)

- 6"× 6" scrap of yellow cotton fabric

- Yellow sewing thread

- Black sewing thread

- Iron-on thread 1/8" ribbon #6240 (Kreinik)

- Teflon press cloth (Kreinik)

- Beads: yellow, gold, and topaz seed beads; assorted medium-size beads and small bugle beads (Blue Moon Beads)

- Gold celestial charms (Halcraft USA)

- Cotton pearl #8, 742 tangerine light, 351 coral (DMC)

- 6-strand embroidery floss, black (DMC)

- Crochet hook, size 0

- Black felt, 1/2"× 2 3/4" piece

- Small iron (Clover Needlecraft)

- Colored pencils (Koh-I-Noor)

- White bond paper

- Aleene's Tacky Glue (Duncan)

- A Fine Line glue (Adhesive Technologies)

- Scissors

- Beading needle

- Embroidery needle

- Embroidery hoop

- Light box

- Pencil

- Black felt-tipped marker

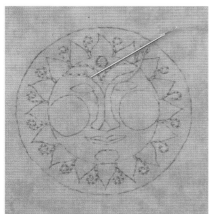

Embroidering the sun

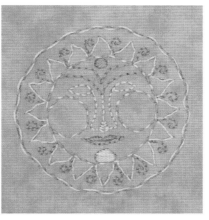

Sun fully embroidered

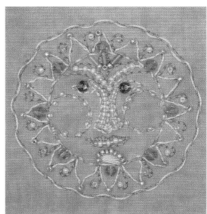

Beading the sun

INSTRUCTIONS:

Cover

1. With a black marker, color the outside edges of the Blank Board Book.

2. Make a photocopy of the sun illustration on page 60. Using a light box, lightly trace the sun onto the yellow fabric with a pencil. Place the fabric in an embroidery hoop.

3. Embroider the sun illustration using back-stitch and tangerine light thread for the nose and sunbursts. Use coral thread to finish the design.

4. Embroider outside of the circle with a whipped running stitch and coral thread; work evenly spaced running stitches around the circle.

5. With tangerine light thread, bring your needle up alongside the first stitch and weave in and out of the running stitches around the circle.

6. To embellish the sun with beads, use yellow sewing thread and a beading needle and sew medium-size topaz-colored beads into each sunburst. At the tip of the sunburst, sew

on gold seed beads. Add beads to each swirl between the sunbursts and around the cheeks, mouth, and nose. Use bugle beads on the forehead and seed beads on the forehead crest.

7. Remove the fabric from the embroidery hoop. Cut out the sun, leaving a $1/8''$ fabric border.

8. String on assorted sizes of beads at the

bottom of the sun. Place two longer bead strings in the middle and two shorter bead stringson either side.

9. Glue the sun on the cover of the book. Using a small iron, attach iron-on ribbon around the outside edge of the sun.

Inside Pages

1. Make another photocopy of the sun illustration. Using colored pencils, color the entire sun yellow. Use light orange and dark orange to color the sunbursts. Highlight the face with light orange.

2. Cut around the outside of the sun circle. Glue into place on the page.

3. Photocopy one of the quotations, trim it, and glue it into place on the facing page above the sun.

Finishing

1. With black 6-strand embroidery floss and a size 0 crochet hook, make a crochet chain approximately 30″ long or the desired length to fit over your head. Tie the ends of the crocheted chain together in a knot; trim excess floss tails.

2. At the top of the back cover, near the spine, add a strip of tacky glue.

3. Place a small amount of glue on the outside edges of the piece of black felt.

4. Lay the knotted end of the crochet chain across the glue strip and place the black felt over the crochet chain. Lightly press the fabric onto the back cover and allow it to dry.

5. Using black sewing thread and the beading needle, sew medium-size beads across the top of the back cover. Sew beads and sun charms onto the crocheted chain.

"Love is like the sun: it has an inner energy source that shines on you."
—Helene Lagerberg

"Some painters transform the sun into a yellow spot, others transform a yellow spot into the sun."
—Pablo Picasso

"Living on Earth may be expensive, but it includes an annual free trip around the sun."
—Anonymous

W is for Windows

"Keys to My Life" Keychain Book

BY KATHY WEGNER

This little book does double duty as a keychain while also showing off your artistic handiwork. The inside pages form the backs of the covers, minimizing the number of pages you'll have to complete. Instead of the key quotes and tags on the inside pages, you may wish to use small copies of special photos or tiny treasured mementos. Feel free to experiment and to substitute other materials for the ones featured here.

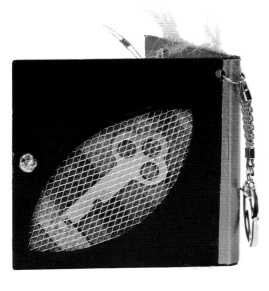

SUPPLIES:

- 3″ × 3″ Create & Treasure Ready-To-Go! Blank Board Book, black (C&T Publishing)

- 4 silver eyelets, ¼″

- White and black alphabet beads, one each of K, E, Y, and S

- Kids' Choice glue (Beacon)

- 2 keys, approximately 2″ long

- Fantasy Fibers glitter Fairy Wings (Art Institute Glitter)

- Mica, clear acetate or plastic, 3″ square

- Super Tape double-sided adhesive sheets and tape (Therm O Web)

- Leather scraps, two 2″× 3″ pieces

- "Key" quotes cut from collage papers or old books, or computer generated

- 2 small silver key charms

- Multicolored fiber scraps, two 5″ pieces

- Incredible multicolored ribbon yarn, 15″ piece (Lion Brand)

- Paragona WireForm aluminum sparkle mesh, 3″ square (AMACO)

- Silver duct tape

- Silver keychain

- Silver jump ring, 10mm

- Silver elastic cord, 12″ length

- Silver bead, 8–10mm

- Access to die-cutting machine, 3″ leaf- or oval-shaped die, and optional 2″ tag die

- Round hole punch, ¼″

- Eyelet-setting tool

- Pencil or pen

- Mini iron or quilting iron

- Ironing surface (covered with Teflon ironing cloth or baking parchment)

- Scissors

- Pliers

The keys to life are friendship, laughter, and love.

Doubt is the key to knowledge.

OUR THOUGHT is the key which unlocks the doors of the world. —Samuel McChord Crothers

INSTRUCTIONS:

Book Preparation

1. Die-cut a leaf- or oval-shaped hole through the front and back covers.

2. Punch four $\frac{1}{4}$″ holes through the front cover above the die-cut hole. Test the alphabet letter beads to see if they fit into the four holes in the front cover—if not, slightly enlarge the holes by pushing in a pen or pencil tip. Push the letter beads into the holes and glue in place.

3. Punch a $\frac{1}{4}$″ hole through the center of each page edge. Set an eyelet in each hole.

4. Apply a $\frac{3}{4}$″-wide piece of duct tape to the book binding. Punch or poke a hole (for inserting the keychain later) through the binding at the top.

Front Cover

NOTE

The clear window, key, and fibers will be layered between the front cover and the second page of the book.

1. Read and follow the package directions for fusing Fantasy Fibers. Spread a 4″ square of Fantasy Fibers on a covered ironing surface. Cover the fibers with parchment or a Teflon cloth. Iron only a 3″ square area in the center, letting the fiber edges remain unfused. Trim the fibers as necessary to fit the book.

2. Affix the fibers to the second page with a double-sided adhesive sheet. Glue a key on top of the fibers and let dry.

3. Using double-sided adhesive tape, attach a clear window (mica, acetate, or plastic) inside the front cover. Join the front cover and the next page using adhesive tape and/or glue.

Inside Pages

1. Die- or hand-cut two tag shapes from leather scraps. Tie bows of multi-colored fiber scraps through the tag holes. Using double-sided adhesive tape or glue, attach the tags and prepared key quotations inside the book.

2. Glue the key charms on the tags and let dry.

Back Cover

NOTE

The wire mesh, key, and ribbon yarn will be layered between the back cover and the previous page.

1. Using double-sided adhesive tape, attach wire mesh to the inside back cover.

2. Apply an adhesive sheet to the inside of the last page and apply strips of ribbon yarn at an angle. Glue a key to the ribbon yarn.

3. Join the back cover and the previous page, using adhesive tape and/or glue. Let dry.

Finishing

1. Attach a keychain through the binding hole, using a 10mm jump ring.

2. Pull silver elastic through the eyelet in the front cover. Pull both elastic ends through the bead and knot close to the bead. Glue the knot and let dry. Trim off excess elastic.

3. Pull the silver elastic loop through the back cover to the inside. Measure the loop to fit around the bead and knot the elastic on the back cover. Glue the knot and let dry. Trim off excess elastic.

X is for X-Acto Cuts

Together with Love

BY LEA CIOCI

The window to your soul, or the surprise inside! Using your X-Acto knife, it's simple to cut a window to showcase that something special in a most distinctive way.

SUPPLIES:

- 6″× 6″ Create & Treasure Ready-To-Go! Blank Board Book, white (C&T Publishing)
- Patterned paper (Provo Craft)
- X-Acto or utility knife with sharp blade
- Cutting mat
- Purple fabric trim
- ColorBox chalk ink, wisteria (Clearsnap)
- Tim Holtz epoxy word stickers (Junkitz)
- Pewter pinwheels (Hot Off The Press)
- PeelnStick double-sided adhesive, Craft Zips, Medium Memory Zots, Memory Tape Runner (Therm O Web)
- Pencil
- Ruler
- Scissors
- Tacky glue

INSTRUCTIONS:

1. Cut PeelnStick to fit the cover of the book.

2. Remove the first protective backing off the adhesive and press the tape down on the cover of the book.

3. Remove the second backing from the adhesive and press the patterned paper in place on top. Trim the patterned paper to book size.

4. To create the window, lightly draw a rectangle on the cover, using a ruler and pencil.

5. Draw a vertical line from the center of the rectangle down.

6. Place the cutting mat behind the cover and, with an X-Acto knife, cut the top horizontal line of the rectangle, using a ruler to help keep a straight line. Do the same with the bottom horizontal line.
Note: Do not cut the vertical ends of the rectangle. These will be the folds of the window.

7. Cut the center vertical line of the rectangle in the same manner as the top and bottom lines of the rectangle. Once all the cuts are made, erase the pencil lines.

8. Open the book and, on the backside of the cover, drag wisteria chalk ink to add color and to show when the window is open. Color the exposed edges as well.

9. Close the window and apply Memory Tape Runner to the back of the cover except where the window is. Place patterned paper facedown so the pattern will show through when the window is open. Press in place and trim to book size. Close the book.

10. To decorate the cover, cut two pieces of fabric trim to fit the horizontal length of the window. Place an adhesive line in each place, then press the fabric trim on top.

11. Add epoxy sticker words to the top and bottom.

12. Add a decorative piece or photo inside the window.

13. Glue the pinwheel accents to the edges of the window opening with tacky glue.

Y is for Yummy Colors

Enjoy Life

BY SUE ASTROTH

It's funny how your feelings can come out in your artwork without your realizing it. I created this book when I was in the middle of several other big projects with looming deadlines. All I wanted to do was take a little vacation and just enjoy life. Well, I guess that came through loud and clear in this project, with all its yummy colors.

SUPPLIES:

- 7″ x 5″ Create & Treasure Ready-To-Go! Blank Board Book, white tag (C&T Publishing)

- Patterned papers: multicolored stripes (Provo Craft); black polka dot (Boxer Scrapbooks)

- Cardstock, light pink textured, black (Bazzill)

- Assorted cardstock scraps to coordinate with the striped paper (My Mind's Eye)

- ½″-wide black-and-white mini check ribbon, 12″ (Offray)

- ½″-wide vintage seam binding, red and pink, 18″ each

- Letters: metal *e*, chipboard *n*, metal *joy* (Making Memories)

- Philadelphia alphabet foam stamps (Making Memories)

- Acrylic paints: red, light green, blue, yellow

- Foam brushes, ½″ to 1″, one brush for each color

- Sizzix die-cut machine, file folder, and bookmark die cuts

- Key embellishment (Making Memories)

- Screw punch or awl

- Red brad

- Red photo tab (Junkitz)

- Thin-point black marker

- Adhesive

- Scissors

- Craft knife

INSTRUCTIONS:

1. Using your favorite adhesive, paste the striped paper to the front and back of the tag book. Trim away any excess.

2. Cut a small strip of black polka-dot paper and paste along the spine of the book. Use the photo as a guide.

3. Using a Sizzix die-cut machine and the file-folder die, make a file folder from pink cardstock. Use assorted cardstock scraps and the bookmark die to make bookmarks of various shapes.

4. With alphabet foam stamps and the yellow paint, stamp the inside of the file folder to spell out the word *life*. Let the file folder dry.

5. With a foam brush, paint the chipboard letter *n* green and the word *joy* blue. Let dry.
Note: Lightly sanding the metal word joy *prior to painting will help the paint adhere.*

6. Using your finger, apply a drop of red paint into the indentation of the metal letter *e*. Set aside to dry.

7. Glue the pink file folder onto the piece of black cardstock. Trim the black cardstock to $1/8''$ all the way around the outermost edges of the folder.

8. Glue the letters *e* and *n* and the word *joy* to the front of the pink folder.

9. With a black marker, write the word *urgent* on the tab of the file folder.

10. Using the screw punch, place a $1/16''$ hole approximately $1/2''$ from the left edge of the black cardstock. Place the photo tab on top of the hole and attach it with the red brad. This will keep your file folder closed.

11. Using the photo as a placement guide, glue the file folder to the front of the book.

12. Wrap both the pink and the red seam binding around the front cover of the book and tie into a bow. Add the key charm to the center of the bow.

13. Affix bookmarks on desired pages of the book so they stick up, as shown in the photo.

14. Tie black-and-white checked ribbon on the center page of the book.

Z is for Zany Stripes

XOXO Ribbon Play

BY LAUREN ASTA

Creating this project is a fun, easy, and alternative way to design a Board Book. For the cover, just a handful of your favorite ribbons—the more textures and colors the better— and a few coordinating embellishments are all you'll need.

SUPPLIES:

- 7″× 5″ Create & Treasure Ready-To-Go! Blank Board Book, white tag (C&T Publishing)

- Letters: 2 Xs and 2 Os, vanilla (The Craft Pedlars)

- Ribbon: 1 yard each of 10–15 assorted ribbons (May Arts, Beaux Regards, Midori)

- Embellishments: miscellaneous beads, patterned papers, and paints

- Adhesives: Wonder Tape (Suze Weinburg), Diamond Glaze (JudiKins)

INSTRUCTIONS:

1. Cut 1 yard each of 10–15 assorted ribbons (depending on width and texture).

2. Layer the ribbon horizontally on the cover until the desired pattern has been created. Make sure that the ribbon spans the entire length of the Board Book when it is open. The ribbon should exceed the length of the open book by 1″ on each side.

3. Cover only the front and back of the book (not the spine) with Wonder Tape. Overlap tape about 1″ inside the front and back pages.

4. Begin layering the ribbon on the front cover. Once the ribbon layers have been secured on the front cover with the ends tucked inside its edge, you can repeat the layering on the back cover.

5. If you want to incorporate beads or other embellishments underneath the ribbon on the spine, string them on after you have attached the ribbon layers to the front and then continue to lay the ribbon layers down on the back of the book.

6. Affix patterned papers to the tops of the *X* and *O* letters, then paint coordinating colors around the edges. Apply the letters to the top of the book with Diamond Glaze

B is for Bricolage

Sisters Niche Book

BY MARY ANN SUMNER

Layer after layer of gesso, paper scraps, beads, buttons, and acrylic paints are added to this artistic cover for a bricolage effect.

C is for Covers and Clips

Autograph Book Necklace

BY PATTI SWOBODA

Covered schoolbook-style with shiny blue paper, this jazzy little autograph book features a necklace made of coordinating blue and white paper clips to complete the school supply theme.

D is for Dimensional

Miffa's Little Book of Fashion Essentials

BY JAN MULLEN

Fabric makes a fun dimensional pop-up accessory to this little book for fashionistas.

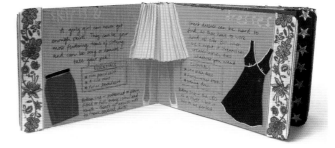

D is for Distressed

"The Places We Go" Passport Keychain

BY DANA SWORDS

The distressed look is created by slightly mixing brown and white acrylic paints and applying the paint with a dry foam brush.

E is for Envelope

Always in My Heart

BY RENEE SAVAGE

The envelope on this heart-shaped book holds a custom ticket designed to admit someone special to a private event.

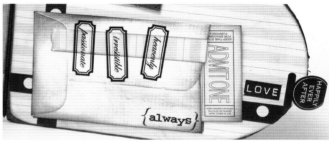

F is for Fabric

Celebrate the Sounds

BY TERRECE SIDDOWAY

Musical note patterned fabric and related embellishments express the beauty of sound as a covering for this Board Book.

G is for Gift Card

Job Promotion

BY ANGELA DANIELS

This unique gift card, made from a tea-bag-sized Board Book, is perfect for holding a bag of your recipient's favorite blend.

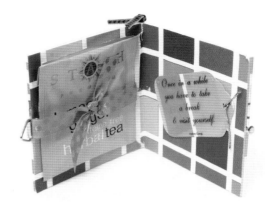

H is for Hanging Charms

Mosaic Journey

BY MARIANNE EVENHUIS

An alligator clip tucked into the spine makes it easy to attach fun ribbons, beads, charms, and fibers to your Board Book.

I is for Insert

Canvas Purse with Mini Wallet

BY JILL JONES-LAZUKA

Turn your Board Book into a mini wallet by simply adhering accordion-folded patterned paper to make the pockets.

I is for Intarsia

"You Hold the Key to My Heart" Keychain

BY STEPHANIE BARNARD

The intarsia (inset) key on the cover was created using a Sizzix die-cut machine and a skeleton-key die.

O is for Opening

Suspended Heart Pendant

BY DEBORAH MACPHERSON

Create a clever heart-shaped opening using a Sizzix Paddle Punch.

R is for Ribbon

Assateague Island Mini Vacation

BY KRISTEN SWAIN

Pull out each tag attached by a ribbon to reveal the story of a fun family trip.

S is for Simplicity

"Tag—You're It" Phone Book

BY KRISTA HALLIGAN

Metal alphabet *tags* and a *tag-shaped* Board Book make twice the statement in this clever phone book.

S is for Stamping

Leather Art

BY ANN BUTLER

Create the look of leather on the inside pages with distress ink, then stamp on your favorite art images.

T is for Tabs

Girlie Girl Address Book

BY JANET HOPKINS

Metal brackets and clear index tabs adorn this hip little phone book.

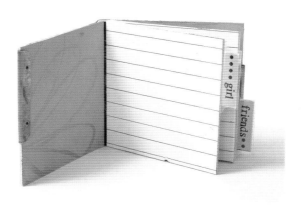

T is for Tags

My Big Book of Tags

BY TERRECE SIDDOWAY

Tags galore decorated with colorful ribbons are tucked into pockets and offer words of wisdom and inspiration.

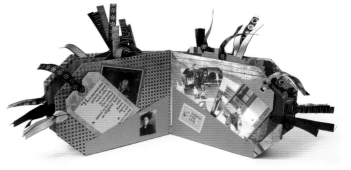

W is for Wings

Inspire Art Doll Muse

BY DEBRA COOPER

This whimsical doll's wings and jointed legs are attached to the book body with ribbon loops.

About the DESIGNERS

MADELINE ARENDT

Madeline has worked as a freelance designer in the creative craft industry for over five years, with many projects published in magazines. She not only designs for companies in the industry but loves to teach others the projects she conceives. Madeline enjoys family life with her retired husband, children, and grandchildren.

LAUREN ASTA

Lauren is a recent graduate from California State University, Chico, with a split emphasis on photography and electronic art. She plans to relocate to New York to continue her art career and while there hopes to experience an opportunity of a lifetime and find much success.

SUE ASTROTH

Sue has been creating art most of her life. A few years ago, a corporate downsizing brought her to work in the crafting industry full time. She has since written four books on fabric and paper arts (her favorite subjects) and has been a contributor to several other publications.

ELINOR PEACE BAILEY

Born in the Midwest and raised just outside New York City, elinor now resides in the state of Washington with her husband, whom she met while attending school at Brigham Young University. Mother of 10 grown children, she travels around the country teaching women to make dolls. "Touching the hearts of creative and loving women has been my greatest motivation," exclaims elinor.

STEPHANIE BARNARD

Stephanie—an author, teacher, and demonstrator—has appeared on the TV show *DIY Scrapbooking* and has had her designs published in the top magazines in the industry. She lives in Laguna Niguel, California, with her husband and two daughters.

ANN BUTLER

Ann has been a freelance designer and teacher in the crafts industry for the past six years. Most recently, she has been enjoying working in mixed media and altered art.

LEA CIOCI

Projects by Lea can be found in magazine articles, ads, and how-to books. In addition to her work as a freelance designer, she serves as demo artist, instructor, consultant, and product developer for several companies in the crafts industry. For 15 years, she has taught at an area college, stamp stores, conventions, and retreats.

DENA COE

Dena has been scrapbooking for two years. Her favorite subject is her daughter; and inking, painting, and sanding are her favorite techniques. She describes her style as "artistic shabby chic." She says scrapbooking is her passion and she enjoys being able to share this with others by teaching at her local scrapbook store.

DEBRA COOPER

Debra lives in South Texas with her husband and two very busy toddlers. She loves to paint, collage, scrapbook, doodle in her art journal, and make just about anything crafty. Her work has been published in a number of popular craft magazines.

LAURIE D'AMBROSIO

After earning her bachelor's degree and having her children, Laurie turned her long-time hobby of making heartfelt gifts into her profession. She has had over 75 of her designs published in almost as many industry publications and is also a certified professional demonstrator.

ANGELA DANIELS

Angela has been scrapbooking since she was seven years old. As she explains, "What really kicked my scrapbooking into high gear was the birth of my two children." She feels that she has found her true style by combining her love of photography with her love of paper and embellishments to unleash her full creativity.

KAREN DESMET

Six years ago, Karen left the working world to become a stay-at-home mom. Now she and her husband have two children and Karen is still at home in Michigan, where she has turned her hobby of paper crafting into her profession. Through her business, she creates and markets stationery and sells home products locally.

SUE ELDRED

For several years, Sue owned her own rubber-stamp and scrapbook store and enjoyed teaching classes. Since closing her store, she has happily worked as a designer for several manufacturers in the crafts industry. Sue lives in Illinois with her husband and three children and loves to create projects in her home studio/office.

MARIANNE EVENHUIS

Marianne lives with her husband and two children in Moraga, California, where she has been creating collages, cards, and scrapbooks for over 10 years. Marianne states, "Altering Board Books has become my favorite artistic outlet. It adds an incredible variety of creativity to my photography without having to occupy too much of my time and space."

KRISTA HALLIGAN

Having always been drawn to art, Krista loves to share her passion with friends and family. She began experimenting with rubber stamping, scrapbooking, and mixed media 10 years ago and is now a part of the creative team at a stamping store in Danville, California, where she also teaches. Her work has been featured in a number of creative paper-craft books.

BETH HOOPER

A teacher's assistant, Beth resides in North Carolina with her husband and their five-year-old daughter. She uses scrapbooking as an artistic outlet, finding inspiration in everything from magazines to song lyrics. Beth loves the variety of paper-crafting products offered today and does design work for several companies.

JANET HOPKINS

Janet lives in Texas with her husband and two children; there, she started scrapbooking about eight years ago. Her passion is for all types of paper crafting and she most enjoys creating projects that her family will treasure for years to come.

JILL JONES-LAZUKA

Jill grew up with a mother who enjoyed crafting. This inspired her to try everything from embroidery to soap making to rubber stamping to candy making. As a musician who appreciates all the arts, she has enjoyed contributing to the memory arts community through design, teaching, and writing.

TAMARA JOYCE-WYLIE

Tamara lives in Grapevine, Texas, the town she grew up in, with her wonderfully supportive husband and three kids. A former teacher and coach turned mom, Tamara now works part time for her father. She is a self-proclaimed pack rat who has scrapbooked since childhood and is passionate about photography.

CHRISTINA KIMMELL

A freelance photographer and mother of three, Chrissy has been scrapbooking for six years. She states, "Creating is a passion of mine—my escape! I get giddy when I walk into a craft store." Her projects have been published in many craft magazines and idea books.

MARGERT ANN KRULJAC

Margert is a freelance artist who loves to dabble in scrapbooking and altered art using all forms of traditional and nontraditional media. Her work has been published numerous times in popular crafting magazines and books. At home in Atlanta, Margert lives with her husband, two children, and two dogs.

ARLINE LOWENTHAL

Decades before the craft world knew of "altered art," Arline was combining a variety of craft techniques to bring mixed-media art to her designs. Although beading and jewelry making are her first loves, she has found ways to introduce these techniques into her art for over half a century.

DEBORAH MACPHERSON

Deborah is a craft designer who never saw a craft she didn't like. She's taught cake decorating, rubber stamping, scrapbooking, metal embossing, origami, polymer clay, jewelry making, soap making, quilling, parchment craft, altered books, tea-bag folding, and crochet. Her designs reflect her varied background.

SHARON MANN

Sharon's passion is designing with needle and thread, but she also experiments with a variety of other creative products. She blends traditional needlecrafts with a range of craft techniques to produce novel, dimensional artwork. Currently, her artistic endeavors include fiber arts, beading, doll making, and altered art.

JAN MULLEN

When not traveling the world, Jan Mullen resides in Western Australia, where she enjoys domestic bliss with her husband, three children, and two dogs. She has a bachelor's degree in arts and crafts with a major in textiles and sculpture. Her family life and quilting business keep her plate full, but she still finds time to teach and write books.

STEFANIE OLBRICH

Residing in Florida, Stefanie started scrapping after the birth of her son in 2002 and has not stopped since. What was once a hobby quickly turned into an obsession for Stefanie. Her work has been published several times in industry crafting magazines and at an online design site.

DELORES RUZICKA

In her flower and craft shop in Nebraska, Delores sells craft supplies and handmade gifts and also teaches classes. She has been a designer for over 20 years, authoring 13 craft books, illustrating two children's books, designing several lines of fabric, and creating many projects published in magazines.

RENEE SAVAGE

Renee has loved arts and crafts since she could hold a crayon. Her current creations explore a variety of paper art projects and reflect her love of art and design. When she's not teaching classes and workshops, Renee enjoys acrylic painting, drawing, and collage and incorporates these techniques into her projects.

PAM SESSIONS

In addition to being a craft/paper arts designer, Pam is a wife, mother, and administrative assistant for a local bank. She recalls, "I have always loved 'crafty' things—from making potholders as a child to making Christmas ornaments with my child." Today, Pam enjoys scrapbooking, card making, and altered arts.

TERRECE SIDDOWAY

Born in Idaho, Terrece has lived in California for the last 20 years. She began stamping more than 10 years ago and now manages a local stamping/scrapbooking store and teaches classes. Terrece loves all things Western, which influences her art projects.

MARY ANN SUMNER

Mary Ann lives in Port Orange, Florida, with her husband, Jeff, two rabbits, and a bird. Her three children, now grown, have been the subjects of many scrapbooks. Mary Ann is a former librarian who now works in an art gallery/frame shop part time and teaches scrapbooking and stamping classes locally.

KRISTEN SWAIN

Living in Delaware with her husband and two daughters, Kristen has been scrapbooking for over seven years and many of her projects have been published in magazines. She states, "My favorite part of scrapbooking is working with colors. Coming up with surprising combinations is one of my biggest joys."

PATTI SWOBODA

Author, designer, and inventor of scrapbook products and techniques, Patti has appeared on PBS scrapbooking programs and enjoys "makin' scrappin' happen!" She loves scrapping with her family and says, "It's a great way for us to connect." As a published author, she continues to create new, easy-to-do projects for others to enjoy.

DANA SWORDS

Scrapbooking and paper crafting have been Dana's passions for almost 10 years. She explains, "My sister and I began scrapping together years ago, before there were so many wonderful products available." Dana enjoys teaching several classes at a local scrapbook store and has had her projects published in a number of crafting magazines and books.

KATIE WATSON

Married to a U.S. Navy pilot, Katie has three children and three cats. She is a multitalented designer who loves arts and crafts and scrapbooking. "I'm also a gourmet cook and a history nut, and I love genealogy," mentions Katie. When she's not spending "alone" time in her scrap room, Katie enjoys teaching at a local scrapbook store.

KATHY WEGNER

Kathy is a freelance designer whose more than 500 designs have been seen in numerous magazines and books as well as on manufacturer websites, project sheets, and display samples. Altered arts, paper crafts, and mixed-media projects are among Kathy's current favorites, but she also enjoys working with wood, clay, jewelry, kids' projects, beads, fibers, paints, and more.

RESOURCES

3M
888.3M.HELPS
www.3m.com

7Gypsies
877.749.7797
www.sevengypsies.com

Adhesive Technologies, Inc.
800.544.1021 x 123
www.adhesivetech.com

After Midnight Art Stamps
866.634.9408
www.amstamps.com

All My Memories
888.553.1998
www.allmymemories.com

Altered Pages
405.360.1185
www.alteredpages.com

AMACO
800.374.1600
www.amaco.com

American Crafts
801.226.0747
www.americancrafts.com

Anna Griffin, Inc.
888.817.8170
www.annagriffin.com

ARTchix Studio
250.478.5985
www.artchixstudio.com

art-e-zine
www.art-e-zine.co.uk

Artgirlz
www.artgirlz.com

Art Institute Glitter
877.909.0805
www.artglitter.com

Autumn Leaves
800.588.6707
www.autumnleaves.com

BasicGrey
801.544.1116
www.basicgrey.com

Bazzill Basics Paper
480.558.8557
www.bazzillbasics.com

Beacon Adhesives Co.
914.699.3405
www.beaconcreates.com

Halcraft USA
212.376.1580
www.halcraft.com

Beaux Regards
203.438.1105
www.beauxregards.biz

Bernina of America, Inc.
630.978.2500
www.berninausa.com

Blue Moon Beads by Westrim Crafts
800.377.6715
www.westrimcrafts.com

Boxer Scrapbooks
888.625.6255
www.boxerscrapbooks.com

Chatterbox
888.416.6260
www.chatterboxinc.com

Clearsnap
888.448.4862
www.clearsnap.com

Clover Needlecraft, Inc.
www.clover-usa.com

Coats & Clark
800.648.1479
www.coatsandclark.com

Colorbök
800.366.4660
www.colorbok.com

Crafter's Pick
510.526.7616
www.crafterspick.com

The Craft Pedlars
877.733.5277
www.pedlars.com

Creative Imaginations
www.creativeimaginations.us

Crossed Paths
972.393.3755
www.crossedpaths.net

Current
800.848.2848
www.currentcatalog.com

Daisy D's Paper Co.
888.601.8955
www.daisydspaper.com

Darice
866.432.7423
www.darice.com

Decal Specialties, Inc.
800.796.8898
www.decorquik.com

DecoArt
800.367.3047 x 3146
www.decoart.com

Design Originals
800.877.7820
www.d-originals.com

Die Cuts With A View
801.224.6766
www.dcwv.com

DMC Corp.
973.589.0606
www.dmc-usa.com

Duncan Enterprises
800.438.6226
www.duncancrafts.com

EK Success
www.eksuccess.com

Elmer's Products, Inc.
800.848.9400
www.elmers.com

Fabricmate
866.622.2996
www.fabricmate.com

Fairfield Processing
800.980.8000
www.poly-fil.com

FolkArt Papier
800.842.4197
www.plaidonline.com

Frances Meyer, Inc.
800.628.1910
www.chartpak.com

Glue Dots International
888.688.7131
www.gluedots.com

Heidi Grace Designs
866.89.HEIDI
www.heidigrace.com

Heidi Swapp by Advantus
904.482.0092
www.heidiswapp.com

Hemera Technologies, Inc.
819.772.8200
www.hemera.com

Hillman Group, Inc.
800.800.4900
www.hillmangroup.com

Hot Off The Press
800.227.9595
www.paperwishes.com

Image Tree by EK Success
800.524.1349
www.eksuccess.com

Inkadinkado
800.523.8452
www.inkadinkado.com

It Takes Two
800.331.9843
www.ittakestwo.com

Jacquard
800.442.0455
www.jacquardproducts.com

John James
800.537.2166
www.kreinik.com

JudiKins
310.515.1115
www.judikins.com

Junkitz
732.792.1108
www.junkitz.com

K&Co.
888.244.2083
www.kandcompany.com

Kandi Corp
800.985.2634
www.kandicorp.com

Karen Foster Design
801.451.9779
www.karenfosterdesign.com

KI Memories
972.243.5595
www.kimemories.com

Koh-I-Noor
www.chartpak.com

Krafty Lady Art Moulds
U.S. Distributor: After Midnight
Art Stamps
866.634.9408
www.amstamps.com

Kreinik Mfg. Co., Inc.
800.537.2166
www.kreinik.com

Krylon Products Group
800.457.9566
www.krylon.com

Lasting Impressions
800.936.2677
www.lastingimpressions.com

Laura Ashley Papers from
EK Success
800.524.1349
www.eksuccess.com

Li'l Davis Designs
480.223.0080
www.lildavisdesigns.com

Lion Brand Yarn Company
800.258.9276
www.LionBrand.com

Liquitex
888.4.ACRYLIC
www.liquitex.com

Loersch Corporation
610.264.5641
www.loersch.com

Loew-Cornell
201.836.7070
www.loew-cornell.com

LuminArte
866.229.1544
www.luminarteinc.com

Making Memories
801.294.0430
www.makingmemories.com

Makin's Clay
www.makinsclay.com

Marvy Uchida
800.541.5877
www.uchida.com

Ma Vinci's Reliquary
http://mavinci.tripod.com/
reliquary

May Arts
203.637.8366
www.mayarts.com

McGill, Inc.
800.982.9884
www.mcgillinc.com

Melissa Frances
905.686.9031
www.melissafrances.com

Midori
800.659.3049
www.midoriribbon.com

Mountain Idea
888.900.2677
www.themountainidea.com

Mrs. Grossman's Paper Co.
800.429.4549
www.mrsgrossmans.com

Mustard Moon
763.493.5157
www.mustardmoon.com

My Mind's Eye
866.989.0320
www.mymindseye.com

NRN Designs
800.421.6958
www.nrndesigns.com

Offray Ribbon Co.
570.752.5934
www.offray.com

The Paper Cut
920.954.6210
www.thepapercut.com

Paula Best
831.632.0587
www.paulabest.com

Pebbles, Inc.
801.235.1520
www.pebblesinc.com

Penny Black
www.pennyblackinc.com

Pilot Pen Corporation
203.377.8800
www.pilotpen.us

Pioneer Photo Albums, Inc.
818.882.2161
www.pioneerphotoalbums.com

Plaid Enterprises, Inc.
800.842.4197
www.plaidonline.com

Provo Craft
800.937.7686
www.provocraft.com

Prym Consumer USA
864.576.5050
www.dritz.com

PSX Design
559.291.4444
www.psxdesign.com

Ranger Industries
732.389.3535
www.rangerink.com

Rupert, Gibbon & Spider, Inc.
800.442.0455
www.jacquardproducts.com

Rusty Pickle
801.746.1045
www.rustypickle.com

Sakura
www.gellyroll.com

Sanford
800.323.0749
www.sanfordcorp.com

Sarah Heidt Photocraft
734.424.2776
www.sarahheidtphotocraft.com

Scrap Village
www.scrapvillage.com

Sizzix
877.355.4766
www.sizzix.com

Stampin' Up!
800.782.6787
www.stampinup.com

Sulyn Industries
954.755.2311
www.sulyn.com

Suze Weinburg (Wonder Tape)
732.493.1390
www.schmoozewithsuze.com

Tandy Leather Factory
800.433.3201
www.tandyleather.com

Testors
800.837.8677
www.testors.com

Therm O Web, Inc.
847.520.5200
www.thermoweb.com

Tim Holtz
www.timholtz.com

Tombow
800.835.3232
www.tombowusa.com

Tool-Tron Industries
830.249.8277
www.tooltron.com

Trimtex
570.326.9135
www.trimtex.com

Tsukineko
800.769.6633
www.tsukineko.com

Two Peas in a Bucket
www.twopeasinabucket.com

Uniek, Inc.
800.248.6435
www.uniekinc.com

The Vintage Workshop
913.341.5559
www.thevintageworkshop.com

Xyron, Inc.
800.793.3523
www.xyron.com

Y&C pens by Yasutomo and
Company
650.737.8888
www.yasutomo.com

Zucker Feather Products
573.796.2183
www.zuckerfeathers.com